ACTING

IN

RESTORATION

COMEDY

Other Titles from
The Applause Acting Series

ACTING IN FILM
(book & videocassette)
Michael Caine

DIRECTING THE ACTION
Charles Marowitz

THE END OF ACTING
Richard Hornby

MICHAEL CHEKHOV:
ON THEATER AND THE ART OF ACTING
(audiotapes)
Mala Powers (ed.)

THE MONOLOGUE WORKSHOP
Jack Poggi

ON SINGING ONSTAGE
David Craig

RECYCLING SHAKESPEARE
Charles Marowitz

SHAKESCENES: SHAKESPEARE FOR TWO
John Russell Brown

SPEAK WITH DISTINCTION
Edith Skinner

STANISLAVSKI REVEALED
Sonia Moore

STANISLAVSKY TECHNIQUE:
RUSSIA
Mel Gordon

ACTING IN RESTORATION COMEDY

by
Simon Callow

APPLAUSE
THEATRE BOOKS

An Applause Original
ACTING IN RESTORATION COMEDY
by Simon Callow

Copyright © 1991 Applause Theatre Book Publishers

Library of Congress Cataloging-in-Publication Data

Callow, Simon, 1949-
    Acting in Restoration comedy / by Simon Callow.
      p.   cm. -- (The Applause acting series)
    "An Applause original" -- T.p. verso.
    ISBN 1-55783-119-X : $14.95
    1. Acting. 2. Comedy. 3. English drama -- Restoration,
    1660-1700 -- History and criticism. 4. English drama
    (Comedy) -- History and criticism. I. Title. II. Series.
PN2071.C57C35   1991
792'.028 -- dc20   91-26381
                                                    CIP

APPLAUSE THEATRE BOOKS
211 West 71st Street
New York, NY 10023

Phone 212-595-4735
Fax 212-721-2856

First Applause Printing: 1991

Simon Callow as Lord Foppington in *The Relapse*.
Directed by William Gaskell, 1983.

EDITOR'S NOTE

Simon Callow was the obvious choice to lead a televised master class on Restoration comedy. He embodies two crucial qualities of that age: relish and articulacy. His two-day class was a fascinating experience, because it opposed the conventional interpretative practice of second-hand flamboyance. With pleas for an intelligent reading above all, he coaxed his group of actors to an understanding of the gusto and fluency that were expected by audiences of the period, and are also essential to vitalize the texts for audiences today.

The notion behind asking an actor who is not a professional teacher to conduct a master class is, first, that the practitioner has authority, and second, that an enthusiastic practitioner will always make his subject accessible, by hook or crook. Theorizing is one thing, doing another. Simon Callow employed some fascinating techniques on his group: playing background music; asking them to imagine themselves very young; making them suppose they were slightly drunk in order to raise them to the "right temperature" for the dense and glittering scripts of Restoration comedy. His methods tuned their minds to both an understanding of the words and of the historical period. As actor, director and writer, he is an accomplished user of several approaches. I believe his understanding is of value not just to actors, but to anyone interested in comedies of manners—or, simply, in theatre: his outlook for drama provides inspiration well beyond the confines of Restoration comedy.

Since even spontaneous speech from Callow is enviably pointed and precise, it has been a delight to organize the transcript of those two days into a book. The television program had to be edited to an hour, but here we can share more of a most stimulating event. (For the edited master class itself, co-produced by the BBC and Dramatis Personae, videos of the ACTING series accompany the texts of this series. Each video shows practical acting technique in relation to a particular medium—such as film; or a particular type of drama—such as tragedy.)

Gratitude for this video/book is due not only to Simon Callow, but a number of others whose contributions were invaluable. First, his class of British actors: Gail McFarlane, Harry Meacher, Pamela Moiseiwitsch, and Michael Stroud. My partner at Dramatis Personae and co-producer, Nathan Silver. David G. Croft, who co-produced for the BBC, and was the program's director. For the script of *The Relapse*, we generally followed the modern spelling of the New Mermaids edition, edited by Bernard Harris. And thanks to Glenn Young of Applause Theatre Books, our publisher.

Maria Aitken

CONTENTS

EDITOR'S NOTE ix
PREFACE xiii

CHAPTER ONE
    Style? 3
    The World of Restoration Comedy 7
    The Text 13
CHAPTER TWO
    John Vanbrugh and The Relapse 19
CHAPTER THREE
    Soliloquy: Act I Scene 1 33
    The Voluptuary and the Wife: Act I Scene1 39
CHAPTER FOUR
    Fops 51
    Lord Foppington's Vowels: Act II Scene 1 55
    Lord Foppington's Character 59
    Asides 64
    Lord Foppington's Logic and Language.................. 69
CHAPTER FIVE
    The Art of Being a Woman 79
    The Use of the Fan 82
    Clothes and Movement 84
    Brotherly Love: Act III Scene 1 86
    Berinthia and Amanda: Act IV Scene 2 93
    The Rest 101

CONCLUSION 103
BIOGRAPHICAL NOTES ON THE AUTHOR 107

PREFACE

When Maria Aitken invited me to teach a master class in Restoration Comedy, I firmly declined. By no stretch of the imagination am I a master in plays of the period: my personal experience of them is limited to one play, *The Relapse*, and, though that one experience compelled me to think deep and hard about the period and its plays, it hardly qualified me to lay down the law about either. Maria explained to me, however, that the "class" was more in the nature of an exploration than an instruction, that it should deal only with *The Relapse*, and that the notion of a Master Class was to be understood not in the sense of a Master handing on his wisdom, but of a collective attempt to gain mastery over the material. This persuaded me, and the following pages represent a condensation of the nearly ten hours of discussion and exploration by Gail McFarlane, Harry Meacher, Pamela Moiseiwitsch and Michael Stroud, led by me.

The Relapse is a particularly suitable play to take as a basis for a consideration of Restoration comedy. It contains many of the themes to be found in the genre, it has a large and varied range of characters, the plot is free of the baffling complexities that bedevil certain other plays (*The Way of the World*, most notoriously), and the language is direct and vital, with none of the convolutions of Etherege or Wycherly. In our discussions, we concentrated on certain scenes which seemed to me both typical and inherently interesting. The result is not a full account of the play, but a consideration of some of its essential elements in a practical context.

Simon Callow

ACTING

IN

RESTORATION

COMEDY

CHAPTER

1

". . . plays, like people, have both a general and a particular character and . . . the particular can only be understood by reference to the general."

STYLE?

Before we try to explore some of the problems, and more importantly, the possibilities that Restoration comedy offers, I'd like to lay my cards on the table. British actors have a very attractive reputation all over the world, particularly for our classical work. We are in touch with this great body of classic drama, unrivalled in world literature, stretching from Shakespeare through Ben Jonson to Congreve and Sheridan, and we are thought somehow to have this work, and the ability to perform it, in our blood, as it were. But, perhaps because of this expectation, many of us are daunted by The Classics. I myself was absolutely terrified at the thought of playing in Restoration comedy. What, me, I thought, treading in the footsteps of John Gielgud, Edith Evans, Maggie Smith? I felt there must be some trick or magic to the delivery of that elevated comic language; that one needed some particular but indefinable gift of personality to carry it off. As it happened—and perhaps fortunately

Simon Callow as Lord Foppington, with Kenny Ireland as Sir
Tunbelly Clumsey. Directed by William Gaskell, 1983.

— my first encounter with the problems and possibilities of the genre was not in a real Restoration comedy at all, but an extraordinary recreation of the genre: a play by Edward Bond called (yes!) *Restoration*. In no sense a pastiche, the play re-invents the language, characters, situations, and even themes of late 17th century comedy. I knew a masterpiece when I saw one, and the character I was to play, Lord Are, is one of the most original and exciting in 20th century drama. But I was completely poleaxed by it. At least I wasn't laboring under the shadow of great predecessors, but I couldn't seem to make the part deliver. Eventually, much aided by the author who also directed the play, I discovered how to make it live. It was with great delight when I came to do my first "real" Restoration comedy, *The Relapse*, that I found I had learned a number of very valuable lessons that made Vanbrugh's play much easier than it might have otherwise been (by which I mean I got further quicker).

I realized that what I had been wrestling with during those difficult rehearsals of *Restoration* was the question of Style. Now style is a much misunderstood, much abused word. It's nothing to do with being stylish, in the sense that Ella Fitzgerald and Borzois are. Nor is it (as we shall see) to do with any imagined period rules of deportment: "101 interesting things to do with a fan." These things may be part of the style, but only ever a small part. No, style is a concrete, a practical, a *technical* term. The best definition of it is John Gielgud's famous phrase: "Style is knowing what kind of play you are in." It draws attention to an absolutely central fact, which is that plays, like people, have both a general and a particular character, and that the particular can only be understood by reference to the general. To do this, you need to ask questions about the world from which the play came, and the theatrical practice of the day. Once you've grasped those general characteristics of the period, the ways in which, as it were, plays from the same time resemble each other, then you can find out the ways in which the play you're dealing with is *different* from all the others, and try to discover the author's preoccupations, and to hear his special tone of voice.

I believe there is a style of playing for Congreve, for example, which is completely different to the style used for playing Vanbrugh. After all, an orchestra plays Bruckner quite differently the way it plays Brahms, though they were contemporaries and wrote for the same sort of instrumental forces. There's an entirely different feel, sound, and texture. Or Cole Porter and George Gershwin: they came from the same period, said the same kind of things, they both wrote witty songs, but there is a world of difference between *The Man I Love* and *In the Still of the Night*. So I don't think there is a style for all Restoration comedies, but I do think that if you work on a number of plays from that period there are certain common factors which make a base for operations. The way in which the language is used, the relish of it, the intellectual energy required to deliver it—these are intrinsic to plays of the Restoration.

THE WORLD OF RESTORATION COMEDY

Literally, "Restoration comedy" means comedies written in the late 17th century, when Charles II was brought to the throne after Oliver Cromwell's Puritan interregnum. Cromwell's Parliament had first closed down all the London theatres, and then demolished them. As soon as he achieved power, Charles promptly licensed two companies to perform, the King's Men and the Duke's Men; both companies found tennis courts as their immediate premises, and began producing plays at a tremendous rate. All the plays were new, and few of them ran for more than three or four performances. The appetite for theatre, denied for so many years, was huge. All these Restoration comedies derive enormous energy from the sense of shackles being thrown off. Far from being prettily decorative, all fans and periwigs and people going "La" or "Stap my vitals," the plays of the period are bursting with newly released energy: the vitality of liberation. Cromwell's reign was, in effect, a cultural revolution, a transformation of society according to ideological dogma, in which the easy and time-honored patterns of life were stood on their heads, normal and natural energies denied and appetites frustrated.

The plays embody the reaction against Puritanism. As H.L. Mencken remarked, Puritanism is the haunting

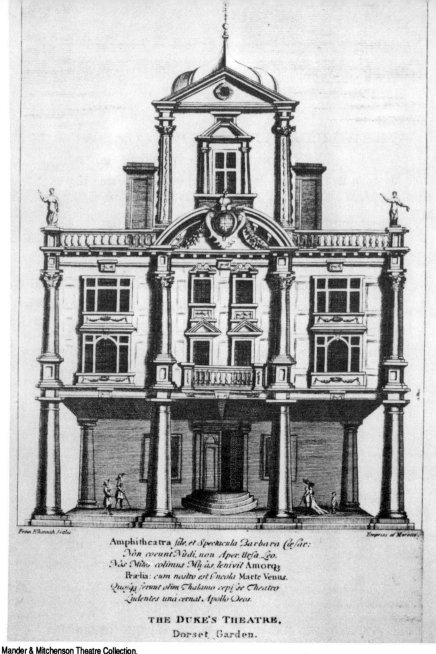

Amphitheatra *file, et Spectacula Barbara Cæsar:*
Non coeunt Nudi, non Aper, Ursa, Leo.
Nos Mites, colimus Musas, lenivit Amorq3
Prælia: cum nostro est Incola Marte Venus.
Quæq3 ferunt olim Thalamo cepi se Theatro
Ludentes una cernat Apollo Deos.

THE DUKE'S THEATRE,
Dorset Garden.

Front elevation, the Duke's Theatre, Dorset Garden, 1673.

fear that somewhere, somehow, someone is enjoying himself. Restoration plays show the society's concerted drive towards what had been denied: pleasure and profit. The plays celebrate materialism and sexual license. They're not epicene in any way. They may contain some epicene characters, but they're not about decadence of manners. They're to do with people wanting things again—having physical, sensuous needs. Money and sex are the threads running through all Restoration plots. They are frequently concerned with fortune-hunting, with people trying to extract money from old widows or elder brothers or to marry into it. The economic motive sings out loud and clear.

The drama of the age corresponded with real preoccupations of the period, and particularly of its middle and upper classes. So the comedies embody values of the court, where men and women of fashion led a life of pleasure and intrigue, disregarding the hated rules of the previous regime.

Fashionable courtiers—mostly aristocrats of independent means—were archetypes for the gallants and heroines of the plays, and the characters based on them were not only rich and grand, but ideally young and good-looking. Seekers after wealth in the plays are typically disinherited, dissipated, or both. Through their envy, these characters also relate to courtly life as a jaundiced view from society at large, hardly able to come to terms with the country's new values.

Reconstruction of Duke's Theatre stage.

The behavior of the court was mirrored on stage. Cuckoldry and infidelity were rife. But while marriage was acknowledged as an unsatisfactory institution, divorce was not the solution. Cynicism was. The prevailing attitude to matrimony is neatly expressed by Berinthia to Worthy in *The Relapse*:

> **WORTHY:** What! She runs, I'll warrant you, into that common mistake of fond wives who conclude themselves virtuous because they can refute a man they don't like, when they have got one they do.
>
> **BERINTHIA:** True; and therefore I think 'tis a presumptuous thing in a woman to assume the name of virtuous, till she has heartily hated her husband, and been soundly in love with somebody else: whom if she has withstood—then—much good may it do her.

The men and women in these plays meet on terms of equality. If the gallants are libertines, then the heroines are emancipated, and can talk freely about love and sex; but ultimately, the women rarely overstep the final barrier of chastity or fidelity, a fact on which many a Restoration plot hinges. This provides a limit to the licentiousness of the gallants, since their women's freedom is only verbal, and female characters generally play the game without paying the price (unless marriage is offered). So the battle between the gallant and the heroine is precisely a "comedy of manners." The language of their discourse followed the lead of the new age too. Conversation at court was an indispensable accomplishment. Restoration courtiers were proud of their wit, loving to dazzle and to shock. Similarly the brilliant exercise of witty speech becomes a hallmark of Restoration comedy.

Since there were only the two small patented theatres in London, the plays were like living gossip sheets for a tiny metropolitan audience, the references lost to no one. Of course the plays frequently transcended that, especially the ones that have lasted, but contemporary gossip must have added great vitality. And any device to hold the audience's attention was crucial. The playhouses were swarming with every kind of activity: celebrity-spotting, orange-selling—and sex. They were centers of operation for prostitutes. If *we* find it difficult to follow the complexity and richness of the language in Congreve, for example, just imagine what the audience of the time had to contend with in competition.

The key to the audience's attention was the acting. Scenery was very simple: a square box with sliding flats to set each scene; so the element of spectacle was small. The players and the play were what the audience had come to see. We aren't equipped to tackle these plays unless we recognize that they demand a special complicity between actor and audience. We have to bring back something of the interplay that used to exist between the two. We can't resurrect the way in which actors provided the gossip of the day, but we can try to recreate the *frisson* that brings. Just like Chinese actors after the fall of Madame Mao, the actors were glad to be there again; glad to be taking their place on the stage after their long exile. It wasn't just the monarchy that was being restored; it was the theatre. All the actors were well known to their audiences. They came on to a round of applause, and there was an immediate intimate rapport. Something of the ebullience of this self-presentation has to be found in performance of these plays today.

Many of the plays share the same sort of plots: seduction, fortune-hunting; and the same sorts of characters: wits, fops, flirts, country bumpkins. There were more than four hundred plays presented between 1660 and 1700, most of them containing these elements. It was up to the actors to ring the changes on these often stock characters and situations. It is the manner as well as the matter that we have to discover to restore these plays to their own vivid existence.

THE TEXT

Restoration comedies demand the most exhausting kind of acting: sustained thinking. Shakespeare with his glorious word-music and the unfailing pulse of his rhythms provides the actor with an emotional wave; the lines have a sort of momentum which bears you along with them. They *give* you energy. But Restoration comedy demands that the brain, as well as the heart and senses, of the actor is fully engaged. These plays live in the play of ideas, which

13

Robert Loraine & Edith Evans in *The Way of the World*,
Lyric Theatre Hammersmith 1924, Wyndham's Theatre 1927.

can only be achieved by thinking through each line. If you do, and only if you do, you will create the necessary energy and lift. You don't have the sensuous, emotional lubricant of Shakespeare's verse to ease your way.

You have to be ahead of each thought, in perfect command of the sequence of ideas. If you aren't you'll be dragged along behind them, and neither you nor the audience will get the images and ideas which alone make the plays so brilliantly funny and apposite. It's like horse and rider, but you can't climb on the back of the text expecting it to sustain you; it will collapse under your feet. The actor's mental energy becomes the horse, and the text rides on top like a jockey. You can never let the mind falter, never lose the energy. But you mustn't be seen to be activating the thought.

Maggie Smith's greatest talent is her ability to think down the center of a thought so it arrives completely fresh. Edith Evans possessed the same gift to a degree unrivalled in my experience. Her recording of some of Millamant's speeches from Congreve's *The Way of the World* is a perfect demonstration of this essential quality. You're so captivated with what she has just said that half your mind is still with that when the next thought comes. The result is that the audience is constantly exhilarated, made to feel fresher, instead of sinking under the weight of a complex text. This buoyancy is crucial; exhausting to do, but without it, you can't play Restoration comedy.

The pace of thought is what creates the pace of the playing. It should not be confused with speed of delivery. Here, more haste is less speed, less effect. Also, many words in these texts have changed their meaning over the years. The syntax has changed too. Modern audiences can get distinctly confused if the actors just rattle it off. If the audience loses the sense of what's being said, then the plays can seem like a lot of people archly posturing together. It's a waste of the rich red meat of these texts.

CHAPTER

2

". . . the problem for the modern actor is the elegance of speech which is thrown over strong feelings like a piece of silk: it has to be effortlessly worn."

JOHN VANBRUGH AND *THE RELAPSE*

Even in the brilliant society of the Restoration, John Vanbrugh stood out: as Captain Vanbrugh, soldier and playwright, and later as Sir John Vanbrugh, architect of genius who built Blenheim Palace and Castle Howard. He was a man of the world, and obviously, extremely likeable:

> I'm in with Captain Vanbrugh at the present,
> A most sweet-natur'd gentleman and pleasant;
> He writes your comedies, draws schemes, and
>   models,
> And builds dukes' houses upon very odd hills;
> For him, so much I dote on him that I,
> If I were sure to go to heaven, would die.
> —Nicholas Rowe (1674-1718)

At the time when he wrote *The Relapse* in 1696, aged 32, Vanbrugh had just returned from a period of imprisonment in the Bastille, having been a soldier during

Sir John Vanbrugh: Castle Howard, Yorkshire, 1699-1712.
North front.

the exile of the king. He was keen to make his mark on the metropolitan scene. He had never written a play before, but two factors spurred on the endeavor. The first was that he was in debt to Sir Thomas Skipwith, Patentee of the Theatre Royal, Drury Lane. Vanbrugh paid him back by resigning his royalties. (In fact, Vanbrugh never made money as an author; playwriting for him was never more than a hobby.) The second factor was his contempt for humbug. *The Relapse* is a sequel to an earlier play by another author, and Vanbrugh reacted very strongly against its bourgeois morality.

The earlier play is *Love's Last Shift* by Colley Cibber. As well as being a playwright, Colley Cibber was the leading Shakespearean actor of his age. Like Garrick and Nahum Tate later, he tinkered about with Shakespeare, altering the text, adding characters and happy endings. (He was also a theatre manager and formed his own company, as did any actor of eminence. It was considered a duty and an honor to do so.) Several of the characters in *The*

South front, Castle Howard.

Corner tower, Blenheim Palace.

Relapse make their first appearance in *Love's Last Shift*: Loveless, Amanda, Worthy (by another name), and most strikingly, a character called Sir Novelty Fashion.

The subtitle of the play is *The Fool in Fashion*. I may tell you, having struggled through it, that it's fairly dull stuff. It's quite stageworthy, but it is oddly lacking in energy and vitality—except for Sir Novelty Fashion, played by Cibber himself, naturally, a brilliantly written and wonderfully funny character, a fashionable fop. It was Cibber's witty invention that Sir Novelty, seeking to outdo all other fops by having the biggest wig in London made for him, has the triumphant creation brought on in a sedan chair—a piece of stage business notorious in its day.

Sir John Vanbrugh: Blenheim Palace, Oxfordshire, 1705-24.
View from Woodstock Gate.

In his prologue, Cibber apologizes for having been a bit near the knuckle in his earlier work. This play, in contrast, is very tame and sentimental. The licentiousness of the stage during the first twenty years of the Restoration was beginning to worry the merchant class: a bawdy lifestyle was not what they wanted to see reflected on the stage. There was strong demand for morally uplifting material, affirming values of family life and sentimental affection. Cibber, ever sharp for the feeling of the moment, obliged with the soft-centered *Love's Last Shift*, in which the rake reforms. He even commented on his change of style in the epilogue to the play, a fairly cynical way of reassuring the audience:

> Such out of fashion stuff! But then again,
> He's lewd for above four acts, gentlemen!
> For faith, he knew, when once he'd changed his
>   fortune
> And reformed his vice, 'twas time to drop the
>   curtain.
> Four acts for your coarse palates was designed,
> But then the ladies' taste is more refined. . . .

Vanbrugh, by contrast, believed in presenting life as he saw it. So in *The Relapse*, he liberates the sexual world of the theatre all over again. It is, of all the Restoration comedies, the one that deals most intensely and directly with sex. Every single scene in the play has to do with it in one form or another. Vanbrugh's frankness

Sir Godfrey Kneller: Sir John Vanbrugh.
Painted for Kit-Kat Club, c. 1704-10.

and impudence delighted more than it shocked. And one imagines even the shockable may have been charmed by his later preface to the play:

> I am insensible of those two shining graces in the play (which some part of the town is pleased to compliment me with)—blasphemy and bawdy. For my part, I cannot find 'em out. . . . I believe with a steady faith there is not one woman of real reputation in town, but when she has read it impartially over in her closet, will find it so innocent she'll think it no affront to her prayer book to lay it upon the same shelf. . . .

It was not uncommon to write a sequel to someone else's play, any more than it is for us to make sequels—and prequels—to films. *Superman II* is a sequel in just the same way: another director and another writer using the same characters. In the seventeenth century, it was quite usual for somebody to take up a character and carry it on in another play, though *The Relapse* is the only sequel of any real note. In it Sir Novelty Fashion is elevated to the House of Lords, becoming Lord Foppington. And, proving that 17th and 18th century attitudes to authorship were rather different to those of our time, the actor/writer/director who invented the character in the first place, Colley Cibber, played the newly ennobled fop, and it provided him with the greatest success of his very successful career. What's more—and this must have been a very gratifying bonus for the now no longer young actor—Cibber is on record as saying that it was very easy to learn: "There is something so catching to the ear, so easy to the memory in all he writ, that it has been observed by all the actors of my time that the style of no author whatsoever gave their memory less trouble."

There are two strands of story in *The Relapse*: one deals with the moral ups and downs of the reformed rake Loveless's relationship to his wife Amanda, and the other, wholly invented by Vanbrugh, introduces us to the country squire Sir Tunbelly Clumsey and his daughter Miss Hoyden. Vanbrugh parried criticism of his construction by replying, "Whether it be right to have two distinct designs in one play, I'll only say I think when there are, if they're both entertaining then they're right, if they're not, 'tis wrong."

The link between the two stories is Lord Foppington, who is rejected as a suitor by Amanda, and cheated of his bride by his younger brother, Young Fashion. But the worldliness of the stories unites them too. Once back in town, and away from his rustic retreat, the newly-married Loveless falls for his wife's cousin, the sophisticated young widow Berinthia. All unknowing, Amanda insists that Berinthia stay with them. Worthy, a young gallant, then starts to pursue the virtuous Amanda, aided and abetted by Berinthia, who would very much like her distracted from Loveless:

Giuseppe Grisoni: Colley Cibber as Lord Foppington.
Garrick Club.

WORTHY: . . . So, good Berinthia, lose no time, but let us begin the dance as fast as we can.

BERINTHIA: Not 'till the fiddles are in tune, pray, sir. Your lady's strings will be very apt to fly, I can tell you that, if they are wound up too hastily. But if you'll have patience to screw 'em to their pitch by degrees, I don't doubt but she may endure to be played upon.

Lord Foppington is also in hot pursuit of Amanda, confident that his recent elevation to the peerage is a passport to "every woman's heart below the degree of a peeress." Meanwhile Young Fashion, having been disinherited in favour of Lord Foppington, impersonates his brother in order to win his fiancee Miss Hoyden's hand and her fortune. She, cynical as all the rest, is quite happy to compromise maritally in order to escape her hated bucolic existence. The fact that she turns out to have got the wrong brother does not seem an obstacle to happiness on her terms.

The Relapse is casual, in the sense that it isn't carefully structured; Vanbrugh was only after a succession of eminently playable scenes. The actors' job was to dazzle sufficiently to disguise the loose-knit plot, and Vanbrugh himself admitted that "The chief entertainment, as well as the moral, lies much more in the characters and dialogue than in the business and the event."

So we have to examine *self-presentation*, an un-fashionable part of the actor's art today. And although the lack of sentimentality and inhibition in *The Relapse* is very modern, the problem for the modern actor is the elegance of speech which is thrown over strong feelings like a piece of silk: it has to be effortlessly worn. Nowadays, the actor has less difficulty in portraying the feelings than in assuming the elegant manner of delivery.

CHAPTER

3

"One of the things I have found useful is to imagine myself slightly drunk before I go on stage—no more than slightly; that lovely moment when the inner and outer selves merge, when self-consciousness disappears, and everything you say sounds rather marvelous—to you."

SOLILOQUY

(Act I Scene 1: a room in LOVELESS's *country house. Enter* LOVELESS, *reading.)*

LOVELESS: How true is that philosophy which says
Our heaven is seated in our minds!
Through all the roving pleasures of my youth
(Where nights and days seemed all consumed in joy,
Where the false face of luxury
Displayed such charms
As might have shaken the most holy hermit,
And made him totter at his altar),
I never knew one moment's peace like this.
Here, in this little soft retreat,
My thoughts unbent from all the cares of life,
Content with fortune,
Eased from the grating duties of dependence,
From envy free, ambition under foot,

The raging flame of wild destructive lust
Reduced to a warm pleasing fire of lawful love,
My life glides on, and all is well within.

Soliloquies are always monstrously difficult. Who is one talking to exactly? In life, one doesn't often address oneself. And yet, innumerable plays before and after the period use this device. How do we deal with it? First, one has to be clear that the text of the soliloquy is crucially part of the action, not apart from it, which means that the character is never "just talking"—he's always doing something—usually to someone else; here, to himself—and that at the end of the soliloquy, he's different from how he was at the beginning of it. Second, one has to establish a heightened mood in order to address the text. This heightened feeling can be understood by thinking in terms of arias in operas—how they stand out from the main body of the action, and are self-contained worlds of sound and emotion.

If Purcell, say, had composed *The Relapse* as an opera, this opening soliloquy would be an aria, alternately meditative and impassioned. It's useful to think about the sensation of what it would be like if you were singing it, first of all because singing demands an element of indulgence—you must go along with the melodic line, be responsive to the color and flavor of the words—but also because there is inevitably a sense of performance in singing, which is also always present in plays where there is no pretense of an invisible wall between the actors and audience and actors. Opera singers have to embrace the conventional nature of the aria. When Figaro, at the beginning of Rossini's *Barber of Seville*, makes his first appearance, he is simply celebrating his own existence, affirming his triumph over whatever life can throw at him: "Figaro here, Figaro there, Figaro, Figaro, everywhere." He doesn't push the story forward, he is introducing himself. But that in itself is a dramatic event, because any story which contains such an ebullient character cannot fail to be changed by him. What's *he* going to do? we want to know. His arrival exhilarates the audience, though he isn't exactly singing the aria to *them*: rather he is expressing his nature in public. The same is true for Loveless: he immediately tells us who he is, and we want to know what's going to happen next.

In playing a soliloquy, then, you're departing from naturalism. To find the energy to lift you up into the heightened state required, you need to borrow some of the opera singer's *brio*. You don't have the orchestra or the tune to give you that: you need to light a light inside yourself. You need to be at a certain temperature before you begin. One of the things I have found useful is to imagine myself slightly drunk before I go on stage—no more than slightly; that lovely moment when the inner and outer selves merge, when self-consciousness disappears, and everything you say sounds rather marvelous—to you.

Music can be a great stimulus for this feeling. I always try to find a piece of music for every aspect of a character, but this is different: here we're talking about music for the scene, for its mood and physical sensation. In rehearsal, this can be used as a background to the speech. Lean on it; let it seep into the pauses; let it feed the sensations. (For this particular speech, I might suggest the beginning of the second *Daphnis et Chloe* suite of Ravel.) Later, it helps to listen to whatever piece of music you have chosen before the performance; it heightens and encapsulates the character. Every night before playing Goethe's *Faust*, I listened to the first movement of the Faust Symphony, which is Liszt's portrait of Faust's character. It plunged me into the emotional excitement and anxiety of Faust's inner self, so that I came onto the stage to utter my first line I had something in my belly; every night before I came on stage as Mozart, I listened to the overture to *The Marriage of Figaro*, and did my best to become it, whirling, gurgling, bustling with irrepressible gaiety, just as it does.

All this is to give yourself a heightened physical, mental and emotional state. Having found that, it is time to think again about exactly what points the speech is making. Simply relishing the language is not enough. Our tendency as actors given a soliloquy is to say, "Ah, a nice long poetic interlude," and to suspend all further thought. Never forget your duty to the line of the action of the play!

To achieve this, as an exercise, try delivering the speech as if it were *to* somebody. If you are playing Loveless, imagine that you are talking to your best friend over several drinks at two o'clock in the morning after Amanda has gone to bed. Then the words will begin to engage. It won't be a poetic wallow, because you have to communicate your thoughts clearly to someone else who might be a bit skeptical. The delivery will come down in scale, but that can be easily corrected once you have learned to present the images persuasively.

A big clue for the actor is provided by the verse form of this opening speech. Verse is a form not much used in Restoration comedy. In this instance, the verse seems to create a certain mellifluousness. It's not very distinguished verse, but it flows. Its mellifluousness creates a certain sensual and emotional feeling: "My life glides by." The combination of assonant vowels and liquid consonants is expressly constructed to introduce us to J. Loveless, Esquire. Loveless *is* that conjunction of vowels and consonants, which is voluptuous, to say the least. His voluptuousness is the rationale for a speech which can be a great puzzle for the actor. The very fact that the verse is not distinguished as verse also offers us a clue to the character: he is neither a poet nor an intellectual, he is simply expressing himself as freely and as sensuously as he can, and yet he is not prosaic. It is an exaggeration of his inner qualities, which are physical and passionate.

Loveless is alone, so he means what he says when he declares his love for the simplicity of country life: he is not trying to deceive anyone, apart perhaps from himself. (The actor, of course, knows from later events in the play that Loveless is quite incapable of withstanding urban temptations.) He tells us that although he once led a rakish life in London, he is utterly happy living a quiet country life with his wife Amanda. As the scene continues, she joins him, and he says to her that despite his contentment, he has nevertheless got to go back to town. She doubts that he will resist the temptations of the city, but he insists that she has changed his character and he will withstand any trial of his virtue. It is a situation absolutely pregnant with danger.

The opening soliloquy of Loveless could be played as if to say, don't believe this chap for a moment. But if Loveless is shown as an enormously voluptuous person, totally susceptible to sensual stimuli, who has yielded passionately to his new love, Life In the Country, the audience immediately thinks: fair enough, but how long before he falls passionately for something else? And the way he describes the things he has rejected is so passionate as to make them seem rather exciting: "The raging flame of wild destructive lust . . ." and the nights and days "all consumed in joy" sound pretty good to me. Vanbrugh might have written a stern Puritan renunciation of city life. But instead, here is a hymn to indulgence. Loveless responds to every aspect of his supposed self-denial with constant physical excitement. And it is comic in one of the basic ways of all comedy: there is a gap between the way the character sees himself and the way the audience sees him.

Look carefully at the structure of the speech. Like so many in classical drama, it is built on opposition. Loveless says, in effect, "I used to be like that—*now* I'm like this." You must sense the oppositions. Antitheses like these are often the driving movement of classical speech: *this* as opposed to that. It is what Joan Littlewood called scattering as opposed to gathering. For example, "The raging flame of wild destructive lust" must be balanced against "A warm pleasing fire of lawful love."

THE VOLUPTUARY AND THE WIFE

(Continuation of the scene. *Enter* AMANDA.)

LOVELESS (*Meeting her kindly*): How does the happy cause of my content,
My dear Amanda?
You find me musing on my happy state,
And full of grateful thoughts to heaven, and you.

AMANDA: Those grateful offerings heaven can't receive
With more delight than I do:
Would I could share with it as well
The dispensations of its bliss
That I might search its choicest favours out,
And shower 'em on your head forever!

LOVELESS: The largest boons that heaven thinks fit
    to grant,
To things it has decreed shall crawl on earth
Are in the gift of woman formed like you.
Perhaps, when time shall be no more,
When the aspiring soul shall take its flight,
And drop this pond'rous lump of clay behind it,
It may have appetites we know not of,
And pleasures as refined as its desires—
But till that day of knowledge shall instruct me,
The utmost blessing that my thought can reach,
(*Taking her in his arms*) Is folded in my arms, and rooted
    in my heart.

AMANDA: There let it grow forever!

LOVELESS: Well said, Amanda—let it be for
    ever—
Would heaven grant that—

AMANDA: 'Twere all the heaven I'd ask.
But we are clad in black mortality,
And the dark curtain of eternal night
At last must drop between us.

LOVELESS: It must;
That mournful separation we must see.
A bitter pill it is to all; but doubles its ungrateful
    taste
When lovers are to swallow it.

AMANDA: Perhaps that pain may only be my lot,
You possibly may be exempted from it;
Men find out softer ways to quench their fires.

LOVELESS: Can you then doubt my constancy,
    Amanda?

You'll find 'tis built upon a steady basis—
The rock of reason now supports my love,
On which it stands so fixed,
The rudest hurricane of wild desire
Would, like the breath of a soft slumbering babe,
Pass by, and never shake it.

AMANDA: Yet still 'tis safer to avoid the storm;
The strongest vessels, if they put to sea,
May possibly be lost.
Wou'd I could keep you here, in this calm port, for
    ever!
Forgive the weakness of a woman;
I am uneasy at your going to stay so long in town;
I know its false insinuating pleasures;
I know the force of its delusions;
I know the strength of its attacks;
I know the weak defence of nature;
I know you are a man—and I—a wife.

LOVELESS: You know then all that needs to give you
    rest,
For wife's the strongest claim that you can urge.
When you would plead your title to my heart,
On this you may depend. Therefore be calm,
Banish your fears, for they are traitors to your
    peace:
Beware of 'em,
They are insinuating busy things
That gossip to and fro,
And do a world of mischief where they come.
But you shall soon be mistress of 'em all;
I'll aid you with such arms for their destruction,

They never shall erect their heads again.
You know the business is indispensable
That obliges me to go to London;
And you have no reason, that I know of,
To believe that I'm glad of the occasion.
For my honest conscience is my witness,
I have found a due succession of such charms
In my retirement here with you,
I have never thrown one roving thought that way;
But since, against my will, I'm dragged once more
To that uneasy theatre of noise,
I am resolved to make such use on't
As shall convince you 'tis an old cast mistress,
Who has been so lavish of her favours,
She's now grown bankrupt of her charms,
And has not one allurement left to move me.

AMANDA: Her bow, I do believe, is grown so
     weak,
Her arrows (at this distance) cannot hurt you;
But in approaching 'em you give 'em strength.
The dart that has not far to fly, will put
The best of armor to a dangerous trial.

LOVELESS: That trial past, and y'are at ease for
     ever;
When you have seen the helmet proved,
You'll apprehend no more for him that wears it.
Therefore to put a lasting period to your fears,
I am resolv'd, this once, to launch into
     temptation;
I'll give you an essay of all my virtues;
My former boon companions of the bottle

Shall fairly try what charms are left in wine:
I'll take my place amongst 'em,
They shall hem me in,
Sing praises to their god, and drink his glory;
Turn wild enthusiasts for his sake,
And beasts to do him honor:
Whilst I, a stubborn atheist,
Sullenly look on,
Without one reverend glass to his divinity.
That for my temperance,
Then for my constancy—

AMANDA: Ay, there take heed.

LOVELESS: Indeed the danger's small.

AMANDA: And yet my fears are great.

LOVELESS: Why are you so timorous?

AMANDA: Because you are so bold.

LOVELESS: My courage should disperse your
    apprehensions.

AMANDA: My apprehensions should alarm your
    courage.

LOVELESS: Fie, fie, Amanda! It is not kind thus to
    distrust me.

AMANDA: And yet my fears are founded on my
    love.

LOVELESS: Your love then is not founded as it
    ought;
For if you can believe 'tis possible
I should again relapse to my past follies.
I must appear to you a thing

Of such an undigested composition,
That but to think of me with inclination,
Would be a weakness in your taste
Your virtue scarce could answer.

AMANDA: 'Twould be a weakness in my tongue
My prudence could not answer,
If I should press you farther with my fears;
I'll therefore trouble you no longer with 'em.

LOVELESS: Nor shall they trouble you much
     longer.
A little time shall show you they were groundless:
This winter shall be the fiery trial of my virtue,
Which, when it once has passed,
You'll be convinced 'twas of no false allay
There all your cares will end—

AMANDA: Pray heaven they may!

(*Exeunt, hand in hand.*)

It seems to me that when we come to play characters, we all ask *who* they are, in the sense of: what are their characteristics? Are they mercurial, or stoical, or phlegmatic? We look for the qualities of their personality. But I think something we frequently miss out on is *what* they are, in the sense of: what is the general group to which they belong? what is the position by which we recognize them in society?—Are they soldiers? Are they wives? What are they? It's very helpful in starting work on a character to find the noun that describes the character, rather than the adjectives. It helps to ascertain what is most important about them. In Restoration comedies this primary definition is generally clear, because the authors deal with stock types. The actor's job is first to identify the type—call it archetype or stereotype, as you please—then discover the essence of that, presenting it in such a way that it is both immediately recognizable (the body language, shall we say, of a soldier) and strikes a general resonance (the overtones, however distantly, of the warrior). Afterwards comes the more complex business of fleshing out the stereotype: giving the character layers and quirks, looking for the contradictions that make up a greater reality.

So, *what* are Loveless and Amanda? What nouns described their essential types? In the first speech, Loveless's soliloquy, we have already seen that the content of what Loveless says is at odds with what he is. Everything that he says tells us that his chief concern in life is pleasure. He seeks sensuous gratification. His principal objective in life is satisfaction. *Voluptuary*—one who wants the gratification of his voluptuous instincts—seems to describe him. That's what he is. We're told nothing else about him: how he earns a living, for example, or what his ambitions or aspirations are. In the rest of the play, he does nothing but follow his physical urges; he lives entirely for pleasure. And yet he preaches fidelity and the simple life. That contradiction is not only amusing, it gives texture and depth to a stock character.

What, as opposed to *who*, is Amanda? She's no prig.

There seems to be a desire on Loveless's part to discuss his appetites with her, and she doesn't seem to mind in the least. She's aware of his interests in other women, and interested in his awareness of her awareness. So she can say to him, "I saw you look at that girl. She's pretty, isn't she?" It's by no means a groin-dead relationship. She's aware of his sensuality, and he's aware of hers. But she loves him; loves their relationship, which is central to her life. Again, we have no sense of her ambitions, her aspirations. She is concerned with maintaining something. She is a *wife*. If that seems a role offering smaller opportunities, think again and try to avoid the predictable response. In plays in which fidelity and infidelity are questions, there is always someone who is wronged. In Restoration comedies, the dramatist is generally on the side of the faithful one—in theory. The character of the unfaithful one always seems more dashing, of course—flaunting morality, bold and sexy. It is easy to see the faithful one as a bore, but we need to find out what Vanbrugh really thinks about that, and what his position is in regard to Amanda.

It would be easy to play wifely disapproval and lose her sense of humor. She has no desire to be a scold or a nag, but she is conscious of his appetite. To show this in her doesn't condemn her; it makes her more human, more truthful, and a lot more richly textured. Finding the archetype is an altogether different thing to playing the cliche. It's important for actors to fight against conventional representation. For example, we may be inclined to play drunk scenes in a way totally unlike the way that we ourselves get drunk—based on a vague race memory of some dreadful music hall comedian of fifty years ago falling about all over the place.

Amanda comes on knowing that Loveless is planning to return to town. The big question is, how does she handle her husband: well, or badly? If we look at the text, the key word is "delight." She says, "Those grateful offerings heaven can't receive / With more delight than I do." I think it should be the clue to our approach. It's very difficult in the 1990s to show ourselves as openly happy. We hedge, we qualify, we ironize. But Amanda is able to say, "I am so happy," without being sentimental at all. It's simply a statement of what's going on inside her: happiness. Because her first speech refers to heaven, it could sound solemn, severe, and "poetic." But it shouldn't. Despite the verse form, it's colloquial language. She's saying, I'd like to give you all the *delights* heaven can offer, rather than, all the delights *heaven* can offer. (It's interesting that Loveless, with his tireless appetite, responds to this by speculating that there may be some new delights *after* death.) It reinforces my feeling about their sexual complicity that he takes her in his arms saying, never mind, we've experienced all the delights. They have complete freedom with one another.

The speech about "black mortality" where Amanda is really saying, "I can't bear the thought of you dying before me," is not a pious thought but a very precise one. Unfortunately, it happens to be clothed in rather elaborate language. It's very important not to collapse under the language, because it's a natural mode of speech to her. People of a certain class and education always spoke in that way—using antitheses, or picking up each other's metaphors—as Amanda does later, elaborating Loveless's "hurricane" with her own "storm" and "port." It's one of the most important aspects of the period that people actually got fun out of manipulating language. They chose to play with words. It's not as if they couldn't express themselves more simply, it is that they got a terrific buzz out of saying it that way. It's like jive talk, or school children who invent private languages. It was a mutual game of 17th century society to talk in that manner. We have to recreate their ease with the language, and their relish of it.

And relish is indispensable to *what* these characters are. There is a relish about being what one is. The stereotypes have to be recognized and embraced before they can be embellished. The starting post for the voluptuary Loveless is his sensuousness; the starting post for his wife Amanda is her wifely happiness. Then there is every room for maneuver.

CHAPTER

4

"Fops are narcissists, not homosexuals. They pursue women enthusiastically, their vanity protecting them from any mockery their efforts receive."

FOPS

We have a lot of handed-down ideas about what Restoration comedies are like, mostly derived from fairly recent revivals. Fops suffer a great deal from this distorted tradition. There is an inherent notion of the fop as a sort of camp clown; an androgynous, grotesque figure. But there are fops and fops. There is a whole range of foppery from A to Z. At one extreme there were the Macaronis, who were a vision of Fellini-like decadence. They were extraordinary etiolated creatures with long fingernails, bizarre footwear and wigs that sometimes stood two feet in the air, so burdened down with exaggerations, both sartorial and physical, they were hardly able to walk. In Etherege's play *The Man of Mode*, Sir Fopling Flutter is a foolish, hysterical fop whose every entrance is a feast of *haute couture*. He moves affectedly as if the floor were "paved with eggs," and his name gives the clue to his flutterings and twirlings. But the contemporary portrait of Colley Cibber playing

Lord Foppington in *The Relapse* makes it clear that he was a relatively unadorned fop. He is a masterpiece of self-presentation, but he's not the clichéd vision of a camp, mincing, furbelowed creature. Fops are narcissists, not homosexuals. They pursue women enthusiastically, their vanity protecting them from any mockery their efforts receive. It was trendy to be a fop, and there were plenty of them. They were confident they were attractive, and there was no anxiety about seeming ridiculous.

Their sartorial excesses must also be seen in the context of the period. Apart from the country bumpkin, all the men in Restoration comedies are dressed to the hilt. The dress imposed certain physical demands. Their lace cuffs made them keep their arms away from the body; their high stocks dictated a proud angle of the head. A gallant or fop had to manipulate a handkerchief with finesse. Management of a sword called for artful flips of the coat, and care in sitting down. Ordinary male movement of the time would have seemed pretty affected to us. In fact, it was a hard-learned accomplishment which men demonstrated with some flourish. Actually, it's only a matter of practice: nobody was born knowing how to handle a sword. You need to practice again and again until it becomes part of your natural vocabulary of movement, just as they did. After all, we know perfectly well how to wear the clothes which are standard for us. If we sit down, men pull up their trousers so as not to crease them too much, and women adjust their dress length according to where they're sitting. Even within the more extreme demands of the 17th and 18th centuries, people were masters of their movement. They wouldn't show it off, they wouldn't demonstrate it; they just did it. They got on with it.

As in ordinary life, when people wanted to make particular points, they wouldn't hesitate to use the wig (or the bustle) to reinforce it. But they were the masters of it. They absolutely knew how to throw back the lappets of a wig in order to underline a conversational flourish, but what we must understand is that there was no code which governs flourishes of wigs and bustles. People used them as natural accessories to their normal human expression.

Wigs were a vital accessory to all gentlemen, but in particular to fops, who could express all their love of excess through it, and use it at least as effectively as another limb. In the famous dressing scene in *The Relapse*, Lord Foppington's periwig is the climax of his toilette:

LORD FOPPINGTON (*to the periwig-maker*): Come, Mr. Foretop, let me see what you have done, and then the fatigue of the marning will be over.

FORETOP: My lord, I have done what I defy any prince in Europe t'outdo; I have made you a periwig so long, and so full of hair, it will serve for hat and cloak in all weathers. . . .

FOPPINGTON: Gad's curse, Mr. Foretop! you don't intend to put this upon me for a full periwig?

FORETOP: Not a full one, my lord! I don't know what your lordship may please to call a full one, but I have crammed twenty ounces of hair into it.

LORD FOPPINGTON: What it may be by weight, sir, I shall not dispute; but by tale, there are not nine hairs of a side.

FORETOP: O Lord! O Lord! O Lord! Why, as Gad shall judge me, your honor's side-face is reduced to the tip of your nose!

LORD FOPPINGTON: My side-face may be in eclipse for aught I know; but I'm sure my full-face is like the full-moon.

But wigs and costumes are essentially accessories; extensions of the character, not its essence. The part of a fop is a glorification of personality rather than a repertory of affectation. Fops remain cardboard creatures unless they are animated by actors. The popular image of *The Relapse* is that it's Lord Foppington's play. In fact he only has five scenes; it's really no more than a large cameo role. But his spirit is its comic glory. He spreads outwards, through his presence, with the most wonderful expansiveness, huge in scale and solidity.

LORD FOPPINGTON'S VOWELS

Before we analyze the first Foppington extract from *The Relapse*, I ought to explain one particular and wonderful feature of the part which looks a bit bewildering on the page: Lord Foppington's eccentric pronunciation. Although it's not written in the text of *Love's Last Shift*, Vanbrugh took the idea from Colley Cibber's performance—he, in acting the part, had invented the idea of Lord Foppington's curious vowels. Was it an observation from life? Was there a fop in town who was crucifying the vowels of the English language in just such a way? Or was it an in-joke? A comment, perhaps, on some other actor's idiosyncratic delivery? The vowels are very precisely noted down by Vanbrugh and essentially consist of replacing an "o" sound with an "a" sound. Perhaps Lord Foppington got the idea from the common substitution of "Gad" for "God" in upper class speech, as in "By Gad!" He says "to tawn" instead of "to town," and "stap my vitals" instead of "stop my vitals." He calls his brother Tom, "Tam"—it's simply an affectation he has decided on. He's determined to impose it whenever he feels like it. It's not consistent. Sometimes he says "nat" for not, and sometimes he doesn't. He does it with complete certainty, having the peculiar gift some people have of mispronouncing words with absolute conviction, as if they were right and the rest of the world were wrong.

I had a conversation recently with a Professor of

English Literature about a program he was going to do for Granada Television in England. Now in England (and indeed in Spain, where the name originated), we pronounce this word *GranARDA*. But my professor called it *GRANNada* throughout, with perfect certainty. By the end of our talk, I began to have my doubts: maybe it *is* pronounced GRANNada, I thought, even though I have been to the place in Spain, and know that the television company was named after it. It's the same with Foppington. He has a certain didacticism. When he calls the restaurant Lockets "Lackets," you feel he's giving everyone a lesson in how to say it properly. It's a device that pays off wonderfully, if you obey exactly what Vanbrugh wrote. He knew precisely what he was doing. When Donald Sinden played the part in the most famous modern revival, at the Royal Shakespeare Company, he made the mistake, as I think, of changing Vanbrugh's vowels; he made Foppington into a *nouveau riche* who said "hice" for house, whereas Vanbrugh has written "hause" and has him pronounce it "horse." "I went into my horse." And it pays off brilliantly in the original text. When Foppington talks about his father having died because he shot himself through the head, he says "Or [our] father is dead, he shat himself."

> (*Act II, scene 1: Loveless's lodgings. . . . Enter* LORD FOPPINGTON.)
>
> **LORD FOPPINGTON** (*To* LOVELESS): Sir, I am your

most humble servant.

LOVELESS: I wish you joy, my lord.

LORD FOPPINGTON: O Lard, sir—Madam, your ladyship's welcome to tawn.

AMANDA: I wish your lordship joy.

LORD FOPPINGTON: O Heavens, madam—

LOVELESS: My lord, this young lady is a relation of my wife's.

LORD FOPPINGTON (*Saluting* BERINTHIA): The beautifullest race of people upon earth, rat me! Dear Loveless, I'm overjoyed to see you have braught your family to tawn again; I am, stap my vitals!—(*Aside*) Far I design to lie with your wife.—(*To* AMANDA) Far Gad's sake, madam, haw has your ladyship been able to subsist thus long, under the fatigue of a country life?

AMANDA: My life has been very far from that, my lord; it has been a very quiet one.

LORD FOPPINGTON: Why, that's the fatigue I speak of, madam. For 'tis impossible to be quiet, without thinking: now thinking is to me the greatest fatigue in the world.

AMANDA: Does not your lordship love reading then?

LORD FOPPINGTON: Oh, passionately, madam.—But I never think of what I read.

BERINTHIA: Why, how can your lordship read without thinking?

LORD FOPPINGTON: O Lard!—can your ladyship pray without devotion, madam?

AMANDA: Well, I must own I think books the best entertainment in the world.

LORD FOPPINGTON: I am so very much of your ladyship's mind, madam, that I have a private gallery (where I walk some times) is furnished with nothing but books and looking-glasses. Madam, I have gilded 'em, and ranged 'em so prettily, before Gad, it is the most entertaining thing in the world to walk and look upon 'em.

AMANDA: Nay, I love a neat library, too; but 'tis, I think, the inside of the book should recommend it most to us.

LORD FOPPINGTON: That, I must confess, I am nat altogether so fand of. Far to mind the inside of a book, is to entertain one's self with the forced product of another man's brain. Naw I think a man of quality and breeding may be much better diverted with the natural sprauts of his own. But to say the truth, madam, let a man love reading never so well, when once he comes to know this tawn, he finds so many better ways of passing the four-and-twenty hours, that 'twere ten thousand pities he should consume his time in that. Far example, madam, my life; my life, madam, is a perpetual stream of pleasure, that glides through such a variety of entertainments, I believe the wisest of our ancestors never had the least conception of any of 'em.

I rise, madam, about ten a-clock. I don't rise sooner, because 'tis the worst thing in the world for the complexion; nat that I pretend to be a beau; but a man must endeavour to look wholesome, lest he make so nauseous a figure in the side-bax, the ladies should be compelled to turn their eyes upon the play. So at ten a-clack, I say, I rise. Naw, if I find 'tis a good day, I resalve to take a turn in the Park, and see the fine women; so huddle on my clothes, and get dressed by one. If it be nasty weather, I take a turn in the chocolate-hause: where, as you walk, madam, you have the prettiest prospect in the world; you have looking-glasses all round you.—But I'm afraid I tire the company.

BERINTHIA: Not at all. Pray go on.

LORD FOPPINGTON: Why then, ladies, from thence I go to dinner at Lacket's, where you are so nicely and delicately served, that, stap my vitals, they shall compose you a dish no bigger than a saucer, shall come to fifty shillings. Between eating my dinner (and washing my mauth, ladies) I spend my time, till I go to the play; where, till nine a-clack, I entertain myself with looking upon the company, and usually dispose of one hour more in leading 'em aut. So, there's twelve of the four-and-twenty pretty well over. The other twelve, madam, are disposed of in two articles: in the first four I toast myself drunk, and in t'other eight I sleep myself sober again. Thus, ladies, you see my life is an eternal raund O of delights. . . .

LORD FOPPINGTON'S CHARACTER

In the scene above, Lord Foppington is doing his social round. It's like an At Home; except it is not his

Cyril Ritchard as Lord Foppington,
The Relapse, Lyric Hammersmith 1947.

home, it's Loveless's town house. But he takes over completely, nevertheless. He is gloriously on display, which is what he's come for. The admiration of his peers in society is his life's blood. It's what he most thrives on. If you tried to crystallize Lord Foppington into a noun to establish *what* he is, you would say that he is *a gentleman*. The admiration of his social inferiors wouldn't matter to him at all. That is why I don't think Donald Sinden's *nouveau-riche* interpretation of the part holds up. Unlike someone who is trying to move up a few notches socially, Foppington has no anxiety whatever about whether he has put a foot wrong. He has seraphic self-confidence. His ascension to the House of Lords is merely a confirmation of something that is already central to his being: natural superiority. What he does is wonderful, he feels, because it is he that does it.

It's interesting that although Lord Foppington's arrival in the house is announced to the assembled company earlier, he is not preceded into the room by a servant and announced formally. It is much more original of Vanbrugh to let Foppington enter unannounced, and just stand there, marinading in glory until he is the focus of all eyes. This is another example of how the actor has to be in a state of high self-definition before he can even walk on stage. When I played the part, the music I found for the character—"The Arrival of the Queen of Sheba" from *Solomon* by Handel—released the right sensations in me, and changed my whole way of being in the role. It's a sunny, ebullient, vigorous piece. (It's what should be inside everyone who plays Restoration comedy.) It encapsulated for me the idea of Foppington as a kind of baroque barrage balloon, who floats on a cloud of ecstasy with himself. He is fully conscious of the splendor of his appearance. When he comes into a room, it's like the Second Coming, as far as he's concerned. He can barely walk, he's so wonderful. And he wants every one to have a proper chance to see him. He wouldn't be so selfish as to move about quickly. Naturally, when he enters Loveless's house, he makes his bow.

Actors always get rather hectic about bowing and curtsying. But in the 17th century, it was as natural to them as shaking hands is to us. So bows and curtseys must be well practised until they are completely un-selfconscious. Every one bowed and curtsied as a social reflex, as it is today, and always has been, in Japan. It was simply part of their natural self-expression for persons of quality. Having said that, the nature of any particular bow immediately communicates something about both the person bowing and his attitude towards the person he is bowing to. Clearly, when Foppington bows to Loveless he's executing a social tactic, saying, "You are not even my equal, but I defer to you, out of courtesy." When he bows to Amanda it is a sexual tactic, saying, "I desire you colossally, and am prepared to defy convention in order to make my views known." Essentially the gesture of the bow would be the same in both cases, but the attitude of the actor, and the way in which he catches the eye of the person to whom he is bowing, creates the difference.

In Restoration society, if I am bowing to a man who is almost my social peer, there is a certain familiarity and ordinariness to the bow, as of long practice. If I am bowing to a woman that I desire, I take trouble to make sure she experiences it fully. I catch her with my eye, make her aware that I am perhaps touching the ground as I bow, and I catch her eye as I come up again, maybe adding a flourish or two with my hand as I go. Neither the man nor the woman to whom I bow would fail to understand the signals that I was putting out. Because the practice of bowing has social formality, it is hard for the husband to legitimately take offence, even though the gesture of the particular bow may be quite explicit to both husband and wife.

Even if Foppington wasn't based on a particular person, he was a familiar type to Restoration audiences: the fop as lecher. There is nothing remotely effeminate about Foppington. He succeeds with women. Almost anyone who is as bold as he is succeeds at least as often as he fails. Elsewhere in the play, he talks about the women he has had, and I believe him. I believe everything that Foppington says. In a peculiar way, there is a sort of luminous innocence about him; a childlike quality. Infants, according to psychologists, experience a sense of omnipotence—a feeling that they are monarchs because they get whatever they want. They are the apparent center of their universe. I howl, and, perfectly on cue, here comes that great breast, glug, glug, glug. When I am finished with it, I push it away in lordly fashion, and then sleep. Lord Foppington's innocence takes the form of never having left that particular infantile stage. So he sees Amanda and thinks, "Ah, I'll have her." He would be amazed at encountering any obstacle to his desires.

When Foppington says, "For I desire to lie with your wife," his delivery of this aside says what he would say to Loveless if he could speak the truth to him. The joke is in the juxtaposition of the public politeness ("Dear Loveless, I am overjoyed to see you have brought your family to tawn again"), and the private bawdy thought ("For I desire to lie with your wife"). The audience is privileged to receive his private thought. This is the essence of the aside.

ASIDES

It is easy to say what asides are, and rather hard for actors to know how to handle them. An aside is simply a moment in which a character on stage leaves the action and talks to the audience. The other characters are not able to hear him—thus Loveless is quite oblivious to: ". . . Far I desire to lie with your wife." The attitude of actors needs to be quite unlike that for bowing, where individual messages not intended for others might be observed by the others, but ignored. The bow was a general social convention. The aside belongs exclusively to the stage.

In a Restoration comedy, we assume that the character making the aside is talking to a contemporary audience of his peers and friends; to people who know all about him and his world. It's a convention that very frankly says, "We're in a theatre." It requires the opposite of the famous fourth wall whose existence Diderot recommended for the ideal theatrical performance: that the actors on stage should behave as if there were a fourth wall where the audience is, as though no one was watching them, and they were simply on their own together in a completely normal room. The convention for Restoration comedies was the extreme opposite. These plays openly concede that what is happening is a selection and presentation of theatrical events, and that the audience, in full complicity, may share the writer's and actors' understanding of what is going on.

In Restoration comedy prologues and epilogues, actors address the audience, sharing confidences by means of speeches that usually suggest: "We are showing you events which you will recognize, and perhaps laugh at. But it is all a play; nothing more than that." During the action, at any moment, any character might step out of the supposed reality of the stage, and apprise the audience directly about something. To serve this convention, the apron stages of the early Restoration playhouses brought the actors into close physical relationship with the audience thus, by design, making asides effective. The settings were simple and formalized: as I said before, sliding flats provided almost all of the stage picture. There was little attempt at illusion or realism.

What the aside demands above all is flexibility of thought, both on the part of the actor and the audience. It pops you out of one assumption and into another. The audience's perception is moved back and forth between the drama and comments on the drama. For the actor, asides can give terrific pace and irony if they are deftly put over, and of course they compel the direct participation of the audience.

The difficulty for the actor is how to cast the audience. Who are they? They are all absolutely different people with different experiences of life. How does one simultaneously talk to them all? How does one find an intimate relationship with them? The simple answer is that in an aside, a character is addressing his peers. He expects to be liked and approved of. Now, the assumption of the aside is always that the character is telling the truth. No matter what he is saying to the other characters, in an aside he always tells the truth about his motives, his intentions and his inner thoughts. So in a Restoration play a character might say: "Good morning, how nice to see you. (*Aside*) I'd like to kick her in the face. (*Resuming speech to other character*) You're looking so well." It is a way of showing the inner and the outer man. Shakespearean and Jacobean plays have the same convention. When a villain informs the audience of his villainous intentions, the audience is assumed to approve of or relish what he's about to do.

Technically, the delivery of an aside is not unlike the way in which non-professionals on television sometimes look into the camera and say, "Hello Gladys, hello Mum!" Suddenly, the distant eye observing them has become a face to which they can address themselves personally. The aside is a frank and personal beam of communication with the audience. It is also a solitary moment, in the sense that it is isolated from the action, though the actor is not on his own. He is with the audience, and— abruptly—completely without pretence. He's not bashing out plot, nor putting over dramatic information. Just sharing his innermost thoughts. It's as though a camera goes into the actor's head and we can see the process of his mind.

Physically, it's usually necessary for an actor delivering an aside to separate himself from the other actors, so that the aside can just flow out, sparing the audience any irrelevant concern about the other characters' ability to overhear. I find it self-defeating and distracting (since deftness is what is wanted in switching the audience's perception back and forth) if the actor steps forward for an aside—with everyone else freezing—then takes a step back. The perceptual jump can be more like quicksilver if the actor is already separate, for some legitimate reason. This raises the question of what the other characters on stage do while the aside is being delivered. It's a very difficult business, because they have to sustain the life of whatever it is that they're doing. They have to maintain their relationships with each other, without enacting any kind of pantomime. It's not a freeze either. Life goes on, but there has been a moment's hiatus, like drawing a breath, while the actor delivering the aside temporarily comes out of the frame. Directors who have characters whizzing about, and special little bits of choreography going on in the background during an aside, are, to my mind, sabotaging the special nature of the communication.

The dilemma for the actors who aren't delivering an aside while someone else *is*, was brilliantly demonstrated in Woody Allen's film *The Purple Rose of Cairo*, when a character steps out of the film into the cinema auditorium, to the sick horror of the cast still left on the screen. In the theatre it's not normally as bad as that, because asides are usually very brief, and can pass as a lull in the conversation for the other actors. Naturally, it's incumbent on the person delivering the aside to get on with it. It's common sense to be quick, with the action being resumed as soon as possible, because a perceptual diversion for the audience shouldn't become a detour over an unsurfaced road. For the same reason, it would be very selfish and foolish to turn asides into show-stopping moments. There should simply be the sense of tossing something out; opening the thing up for a second.

LORD FOPPINGTON'S LOGIC AND LANGUAGE

You might expect Lord Foppington's arrival to be a cue for us to mock him. But it doesn't happen like that. Lord Foppington is so sublimely sure of himself that he takes complete control of the scene. He has a small brain, perhaps; he certainly has a small range of subjects about which he thinks; but when I played him, it came to be my belief that he was a genius. He applies a laser-like intellect to the few matters which concern him. Almost everything he says in the scene is sententious. He makes judgements. From his position of enormous self-confidence, he tells his friends on stage and in the audience the truth about his life.

He is sure that he is the greatest conversationalist of the age, and that people hang on his every word. Edward Bond acutely described the patterns of thought of his character Lord Are in *Restoration*. "Lord Are," he said, "is never speculative." Neither is Lord Foppington. He never teeters towards an idea, he always hits it bang on the head. And however Alice-in-Wonderland his logic is, it *is* logic. The construction of his exchange with Amanda is a beautiful syllogism. It is unarguable. The logic is ironclad. He says country life is fatiguing; she says it's quiet. He says quietness is fatiguing because it's impossible to be quiet without thinking. Q.E.D.: thinking is fatiguing.

Amanda changes tack, for you can never confound Lord Foppington's logic. You have to give in or go mad. He is a principle of anarchy in the play because he follows his own line unswervingly through it, and others simply have to jump out of the way. Amanda says, "Don't you like to read when things are quiet?" Foppington says, "Oh yes, but I don't think about what I read." Berinthia chips in with the obviously sensible challenge, "*Can* you read without thinking?" Foppington replies, "Can you pray without devotion?" Round Two to Lord Foppington. It is perfectly possible to go through the form of praying without genuine religious experience, so why should he think when he's reading? And, it is a rather outrageous thing to say. Only twenty years before, England had been absolutely in the hands of the repressively religious Puritans. The audience probably shared Foppington's view, though it was still quite a shocking thought to voice. Foppington is outrageous, but he hasn't got an ounce of hypocrisy.

Dealing with Foppington is like dealing with a convinced Marxist. When you are challenging a really clever dialectical thinker, you've got to go back to his first proposition or you can never win an argument. The challenges offered by the other characters in this scene are intelligent challenges. The intelligence of everyone on stage is one of the prime qualities of the scene. Like all the notions expressed in Restoration comedy, these must be held up for our inspection. We must hear the concept, know what Foppington thinks about it, what Amanda thinks, what Berinthia. The characters are thinking people, and the actors playing them must display the same flexibility of mind.

When Foppington describes his gallery of books and looking-glasses: "Madam, I have gilded 'em, and ranged 'em so prettily, before Gad, it is the most entertaining thing in the world to walk and look upon 'em," and with brilliant wit, expresses his pleasure in seeing himself reflected. For these brilliant comic images to register, the actor has to make the audience see what he is describing. The danger of comedy of language is that the brilliant, colorful words can seduce the actor into mere rhythms and inflections. The actor can fall in love with the shapes of the language. But, it's a *picture* you're supposed to be *drawing*. A picture. If you get the narrative right, you tell the story, and you must tell the story with the picture, as per the script. Every story, to invert the newspaperman's cliché, tells a picture. It's a sequence of images you are offering the audience, and they must see them clearly. They can only see them if the actor sees them.

To continue with the scene: Amanda makes another assault on Lord Foppington's thought processes when she delicately suggests that perhaps the inside of a book is more important than its binding. An unexceptionable point of view—but Lord Foppington completely rejects it. He says, in effect, I don't think one should read books, because other people's ideas interfere with one's originality. A radical idea, but an *arguable* one. We all know people who are so crammed with this person's theory and that person's book that they hardly know what they think themselves. Almost everything Lord Foppington says is defensible.

When Lord Foppington reveals the details of his daily life to the company, he never doubts for an instant that they are of supreme interest. It is as if there was an enormous store of self-evident truth in him which he graciously dispenses to those lucky enough to be around. "I don't rise sooner because it's the worst thing in the world for the complexion": it's his saying for the day. There is the feeling of, "You can quote me on this."

So the delivery requires the seriousness of weighty matters, despite the trivial content. Foppington is totally serious about all matters relating to himself. He would never joke about something so supremely important. If he were a satirist, he might make a witty comment about the fact that audiences never look at the play, they look at each other. But his way of putting it is from Foppington's angle, an inverted point of view: ". . . a man must endeavour to look wholesome, lest he make so nauseous a figure in the side-bax, the ladies should be compelled to turn their eyes upon the play." It is a joke for us (and more humorous this way round), but

Sir John Vanbrugh: Blenheim Palace, Oxfordshire, 1705-24.
North front from the garden bridge.

Courtesy Nathan Silver.

it is deadly serious for Foppington.

The inquiry about whether he is tiring the company with his account of his day is merely rhetorical. It's a piece of punctuation, no more, for Lord Foppington has not the smallest intention of stopping. The reference to "Lacket's" is topical: Locket's was a fashionable restaurant of the day. But luckily the joke transcends time barriers. It is still applicable to *nouvelle cuisine* establishments where they give you a dish the size of a thimble and charge you a fortune, and everyone goes into fashionable ecstasies.

Foppington expresses himself, or certainly intends to express himself, in epigrammatic form. An epigram is different in form and feeling from simple wit. There is always a paradox at the centre of an epigram: an inversion of commonly perceived reality. There is, too, a sense of authoritativeness about them; a judgement, something summed up for good and all. Remarks like: ". . . Far to my mind, the inside of a book is to entertain one's self with the forced product of another man's brain. Naw I think a man of quality and breeding may be much better diverted with the natural sprauts of his own"—need to be *announced*. They need to be *propounded*. Being *said* just won't do. These texts are lapidary. The words are almost chiselled on stone.

Edith Evans had the great gift of articulating each phase of thought in an epigram almost as if she were placing it on a shelf in front of her. Then she would add the next section, and then the one after it, and then the final one to make up the whole idea, which would then sit on this shelf in the air, clearly visible. We can still hear it in the recording she made of some scenes from *The Way of the World* in which she played, at different times of her life, Millamant and Lady Wishfort. The epigrams seem to hover in space, and however complicated the sequence of thought, you see every thing she's talking about. She gave each phrase its full value, which requires continuous thinking. You can't anticipate; you can't look back; you must think each thought *now* as you utter it. You can't rely on the words themselves to do the work for you. The thoughts have to be presented, properly held up for our inspection. It's an entirely different sensation from the way we usually phrase. We normally find the centre of a phrase, build up to it, and fall away again. But an epigram is an arch of bricks, ingeniously put in place without support, until the last brick holds it all up.

There is no one quite like Lord Foppington in the other Restoration comedies. He is irresistible because he is a sunny man; a man of no melancholy, no distress, no self-doubt, and no real malice either. He has a vast and radiant self-confidence. He makes me think of another of Vanbrugh's great creations: Blenheim Palace. He has a stately expansive rhythm of his own which is built into the text, as long as the ideas are not skated over.

CHAPTER

5

"In the Restoration theatre, actresses seized their opportunity and found a million different ways of revealing and demonstrating what it was to be a woman."

THE ART OF BEING A WOMAN

Restoration comedy celebrates femininity. For audiences of the Restoration period, the revelation of women on the stage was a kind of witchcraft; a tremendous sexual energy and power. Previously, boys had impersonated women; but in 1662, Charles II issued a royal patent which permitted women to appear on the English stage for the very first time. The effect must have been like the first tentative admission—only a very few years ago—of girls into certain English public schools: the whole atmosphere became sexualized in an entirely new way. In the Restoration theatre, actresses seized their opportunity and found a million different ways of revealing and demonstrating what it was to be a woman. So in the plays of the period, partly because actresses were so unfamiliar to audiences, and partly because they revealed new aspects of womanliness, every encounter between a man and a woman on stage becomes an archetypal encounter between the masculine principle and the

Restoration dress. Sir Peter Lely: *Two Ladies of the Lake Family*.

feminine principle. Sex was everywhere.

To recapture this in more modern times can be tricky. Women have well and truly claimed their position in the theatre, as writers, directors, managers (Gladys Cooper's company in the '20s was one of the glories of the age) as well as actresses. The novelty has, to say the least, worn off. In addition to this, in our age, the transformation in sexual politics has called into question the very notion of celebrating femininity: is that not merely another form of oppression, by which women are obliged to behave according to men's definition, satisfying men's fantasies and requirements? This is a very new development, and carries with it, as usual in any ideological breakthrough, a complex mix of gains and losses. What is certain, though, is that the dramatists of the Restoration, both men and women, were far from being feminists. In order to play their characters and understand their plays, we have to take into account the context in which both existed, and one of the central ingredients was the opportunity for a much more dangerous sort of sexual by-play than had hitherto been seen on the English stage; and central to that was the *frisson* caused by the arrival of women with all their erotic potential into a hitherto all-male enclave.

The magic of women, their ju-ju, was, again until very recently, one of the great branches of theatrical art: their clothes, their physical movement, the tricks, as it were, of their trade, were studied and perfected not only by the actresses themselves—who acquired astonishing expertise in creating their effects within a tiny range of permitted behavior—but by their directors. As recently as 1951, when Laurence Olivier directed and played opposite Vivien Leigh in Rattigan's *The Sleeping Prince*, it was observed by a critic that every time Miss Leigh came on to the stage it seemed to light up. But it didn't just *seem* to light up, it actually did. All the lights went up a few points whenever Vivien Leigh walked on stage, and they went down again when she left it. It sounds like egomania run rampant, but it wasn't; it was a way of enhancing the kind of witchcraft her character represented, the million ways of being a woman.

In old films you can see the lighting of a cigarette

by, say, a Bette Davis or an Ingrid Bergman, as an opportunity to crystallize aspects of desire. We tend to dismiss that sort of thing nowadays as rather stagy, rather self-conscious, but it is an equivalent of the Restoration's armory of feminine tricks. And think of the scene in Anita Loos' play *Gigi* where the old grandmother teaches Gigi how to use jewels. "You must wear it here if you want a certain effect on a man, and you must wear it there if you want another effect." In Restoration comedy it is not enough simply to be a woman, the actress has to give an *exhibition* of being a woman.

THE USE OF THE FAN

The use of the fan, far from being an arbitrary affectation, was part of the enormous repertory of a woman's wiles. Their use was inherited wisdom; one can imagine a mother teaching her daughter: "Darling, never open your fan like that, let it out very gently." It was not an accessory like a parasol or a muff. It was an indispensable adjunct to social life, because it spoke a language of its own. I don't mean any sort of decorous Japanese-like "language of the fan," where each position has attributed to it some precise meaning; but a subtext language, where the fan can improvise, sometimes faster than the tongue, sometimes merely saying a bit more than the tongue. It's what provoked that interesting remark of Edith Evans that you can do almost anything with a fan except fan yourself with it. This speech from Cibber's

A Restoration fan. Ivory fan, c. 1690-1700, French.
The leaf is painted with ladies, gallants and *putti* playing
before a view of the gardens of Versailles; in the center
a lady at her dressing table is taking a pinch of snuff.

Love's Last Shift shows perfectly how a fan reinforces
a coquette's weaponry:

> Why, madam, I have observed several particular
> qualities in your ladyship that I have perfectly adored
> you for; as, the majestic toss of your head;—your
> obliging bow-curtsey;—your demure look;—the
> careless tie of your hood;—the genteel flirt of your
> fan;—the designed accident in your letting it fall,
> and your agreeable manner of receiving it from him
> that takes it up.

CLOTHES AND MOVEMENT

It's not the human body that's changed, it is the clothes. I don't think there's really such a thing as "period movement." The clothes dictate the movement. Every character in a Restoration comedy lived and breathed in those clothes. We must try to imagine what difference to their lives it made to wear a bustle, a wig, a corset. Seventeenth century ladies wore stays, so their backs were straight and it was more comfortable to sit on the edge of a chair. Long skirts need kicking out in front so as not to tread on them—which is why Athene Seyler told actresses to "dance" in Restoration costume. If a costume has a train, then a wide turning circle is needed, and other performers must be aware of this need. A sudden turn has to be achieved with a backwards kick to get the train out of the way. It can be a very effective form of punctuation. The point is, the clothes must work for you, not against you. Restoration actresses used them as part of their formidable display techniques, never wasting the swing of a skirt or the sway of a ruffle. In rehearsal, it is advisable to mock up as much of your costume as you can, so that nothing takes you by surprise and every bobbing feather can be exploited on stage. And cleavage is a necessity. The 17th century silhouette wasn't achieved without artifice. Never be ashamed to heave and pad.

Restoration dress. Studio of Sir Peter Lely: Nell Gwyn, c. 1675.

BROTHERLY LOVE

(Act III scene 1)

YOUNG FASHION: Brother, though I know to talk to you of business (especially of money) is a theme not quite so entertaining to you as that of the ladies, my necessities are such, I hope you'll have patience to hear me.

LORD FOPPINGTON: The greatness of your necessities, Tam, is the worst argument in the world for your being patiently heard. I do believe you are going to make me a very good speech, but, strike me dumb! it has the worst beginning of any speech I have heard this twelvemonth.

YOUNG FASHION: I'm very sorry you think so.

LORD FOPPINGTON: I do believe thau art. But come, let's know thy affair quickly; far 'tis a new play, and I shall be so rumpled and squeezed with pressing through the crawd, to get to my servant, the women will think I have lain all night in my clothes.

YOUNG FASHION: Why, then (that I may not be the author of so great a misfortune) my case in a word is this. The necessary expenses of my travels have so much exceeded the wretched income of my annuity, that I have been forced to mortgage it for five hundred pounds, which is spent; so that unless you are so kind to assist me in redeeming it, know no remedy but to go take a purse.

LORD FOPPINGTON: Why, faith, Tam—to give you my sense of the thing, I do think taking a purse is the best remedy in the world: for if you succeed, you are relieved that way; if you are taken—you are relieved t'other.

YOUNG FASHION: I'm glad to see you are in so pleasant a humor. I hope I shall find the effects on't.

LORD FOPPINGTON: Why, do you then really think it a reasonable thing I should give you five hundred paunds?

YOUNG FASHION: I do not ask it as a due, brother, I am willing to receive it as a favor.

LORD FOPPINGTON: Thau art willing to receive it anyhaw, strike me speechless! But these are damned times to give money in, taxes are so great, repairs are so exorbitant, tenants such rogues, and periwigs so dear, that the devil take me, I am reduced to that extremity in my cash, I have been forced to retrench in that one article of sweet pawder, till I have braught it dawn to five guineas a manth. Naw judge, Tam, whether I can spare you five hundred paunds.

YOUNG FASHION: If you can't, I must starve, that's all.—(*Aside*) Damn him!

LORD FOPPINGTON: All I can say is, you should have been a better husband.

YOUNG FASHION: Oons, if you can't live upon five thousand a year, how do you think I should do't upon two hundred?

LORD FOPPINGTON: Don't be in a passion, Tam; far passion is the most unbecoming thing in the world—to the face. Look you, I don't love to say anything to you to make you melancholy; but upon this occasion I must take leave to put you in mind that a running horse does require more attendance than a coach-horse. Nature has made some difference 'twixt you and I.

YOUNG FASHION: Yes, she has made you older—(*Aside*) Pox take her!

LORD FOPPINGTON: That is nat all, Tam.

YOUNG FASHION: Why, what is there else?

LORD FOPPINGTON (*Looking first upon himself, then upon his brother*) Ask the ladies.

YOUNG FASHION: Why, thou essence bottle! thou musk cat! dost thou then think thou hast any advantage over me but what Fortune has given thee?

LORD FOPPINGTON: I do—stap my vitals!

YOUNG FASHION: Now, by all that's great and powerful, thou art the prince of coxcombs!

LORD FOPPINGTON: Sir—I am praud of being at the head of so prevailing a party.

YOUNG FASHION: Will nothing then provoke thee? Draw, coward!

LORD FOPPINGTON: Look you, Tam, you know I have always taken you for a mighty dull fellow, and here is one of the foolishest plats broke out that I have seen a long time. Your paverty makes your life so burdensome to you, you would provoke me to a quarrel, in hopes either to slip through my lungs into my estate, or to get yourself run through the guts, to put an end to your pain. But I will disappoint you in both your designs; far, with the temper of a philasapher, and the discretion of a statesman—I will go to the play with my sword in my scabbard. (*Exit*)

YOUNG FASHION: Sooh! Farewell, snuff-box! And now, conscience, I defy thee.—Lory!

The Relapse links two sexual plots: Loveless's pursuit of Berinthia (and hers of him) and Young Fashion's pursuit of Hoyden. The connection is Lord Foppington, who is Loveless's friend (he makes an outrageously misjudged attempt to seduce Loveless's wife, Amanda), and who is contracted to marry the (as yet unseen) Hoyden. But the pivot of the second plot is Young Fashion, Foppington's younger brother. Rendered penniless by the law of primogeniture (by which the oldest son inherits the father's entire estate) he decides to highjack his brother's bride-to-be, and by marrying her, win her fortune. He thus combines three important figures of Restoration comedy: the leading young man, or *jeune premier*; the dispossessed younger son; and the fortune hunter trying to make a rich marriage.

The young romantic lead is to be found in plays of many periods, but the part offers great difficulties for us today. The condition of being young has changed radically, and though it is to be doubted whether human nature has fundamentally changed, it is rare nowadays to find people of their late teens and early twenties who present themselves with unaffected, open-faced simplicity—glad to be young and alive, as it were. Once again, it should be stressed that nobody ever was *that* uncomplicated, but this simplicity was an assumption for the sake of presenting a normal mode, and it is usually the normal mode that is the starting-point for classical dramatists.

Young Fashion has no character to speak of. He is lively, impulsive, good-natured; but angry about his ill-usage at the hands of his brother. In all of this he has much in common with Orlando in *As You Like It*. The two parts present similar difficulties. It would be a bad mistake to try to endow Fashion (or Orlando) with complexes, or "interesting" characteristics. The important thing to latch on to is youthfulness. (This was so clearly understood to be the case in the 17th century that the part was played by a woman—a conventional way of saying, "this character is young." The convention is to be found most commonly in opera, with Cherubino in *The Marriage of Figaro* and Octavian in *Der Rosenkavalier* both being sung by women.)

The actor needs to find his own youthfulness and bring that as simply and boldly as possible on stage. The audience should be attracted to, and be rooting for, the juvenile lead. The same figure appears in the old Roman comedies. In a comedy, the audience is always presumed to be on the side of youth and against age.

In the section that precedes the extract above,

Foppington outrages Fashion with his cynically self-centred view of sex. Fashion is not a wimp, but he has idealistic views. He has not yet worked out how to turn the world to his advantage. This aspect of the character may not strike the actor as very rewarding, but it is essential for the success of the play that the elements of youth, hope and innocence should be established as strongly and clearly as possible. Their triumph (however wittily qualified) is a big part of the resolution of the play.

Foppington and Fashion have two big confrontations in the play. Both hinge on money. Foppington refuses to acknowledge any obligation to provide Fashion with money, though he will (in the first scene) give him a meal:

> FOPPINGTON: If you'll stay here, you'll find a family dinner—Hey fellow! What is there for dinner? There's beef: I suppose my brother will eat beef. Dear Tam I' glad to see thee in England, stap my vitals! (*Exit with his equipage*)

In their second confrontation, Fashion is more determined, less easily deflected. But Foppington is more than a match for him, provoking him with his languid wit and lack of even ordinary consideration to wild rage and rash gestures. Again, Foppington perfectly undercuts him by refusing to engage him in a duel:

> FOPPINGTON: ... far, with the temper of a philasapher,

and the discretion of a statesman—I will go to the
play with my sword in my scabbard.

It is important to sense how deep Fashion's frustration
and fury are. Quite apart from his own understandable
anger, he belonged to a recognized group with a grievance:
younger brothers. The law of primogeniture was a
relatively recent innovation in English law, dating from
the early Elizabethan period. It was introduced by a
bourgeoisie anxious to consolidate its family wealth,
not dissipate it by dividing it up at death. There were
literally thousands of younger brothers roaming the land
with no money and nothing to do. Many—like
Fashion—went abroad, soldiering. Others stayed at home
and tried to make a good marriage. Young Fashion's
needs are very real.

His quest for a bride—which has the gratifying double
effect of winning him capital and cheating his brother—has no romantic dimension to it whatever. He hasn't
even seen the girl, any more than has Foppington. But
(again, a common element in these plays), once he sees
the girl, he is roused, and his desire for her becomes
almost as strong a motive as the money and the revenge.
It is very important, though, that both the fortune-hunting
and the rage of the younger brother should be played
for all they're worth, not only for the purposes of the
plot—to which they're essential—nor because the more
seriously they're played, the funnier the play will be;

but for the sake of Young Fashion himself, who can easily become a lightweight character, but who is in fact one of the most attractive, strongest and most vivacious of them all.

BERINTHIA AND AMANDA

(Act IV, scene 2: Loveless's lodgings. Enter AMANDA *and* BERINTHIA.)

AMANDA: Well, now, Berinthia, I'm at leisure to hear what t'was you had to say to me.

BERINTHIA: What I had to say was only to echo the sighs and groans of a dying lover.

AMANDA: Phu! will you never learn to talk in earnest of anything?

BERINTHIA: Why this shall be in earnest, if you please. For my part, I only tell you matter of fact, you may take it which way you like best; but if you'll follow the women of the town, you'll take it both ways; for when a man offers himself to one of them, first she takes him in jest, and then she takes him in earnest.

AMANDA: I'm sure there's so much jest and earnest in what you say to me, I scarce know how to take it; but I think you have bewitched me, for I don't find it possible to be angry with you, say what you will.

BERINTHIA: I'm very glad to hear it, for I have no mind to quarrel with you, for more reasons than I'll brag of; but quarrel or not, smile or frown, I must tell you what I have suffered upon your account.

AMANDA: Upon my account?

BERINTHIA: Yes, upon yours; I have been forced to sit still and hear you commended for two hours together, without one compliment to myself; now don't you think a woman had a blessed time of that?

AMANDA: Alas! I should have been unconcerned at it; I never knew where the pleasure lay of being praised by the men. But pray who was it that commended me so?

BERINTHIA: One you have a mortal aversion to, Mr. Worthy; he used you like a text, he took you all to pieces, but spoke so learnedly on every point, one might see the spirit of the church was in him. If you are a woman, you'd have been in an ecstasy to have heard how feelingly he handled your hair, your eyes, your nose, your mouth, your teeth, your tongue, your chin, your neck, and so forth. Thus he preached for an hour, but when he came to use an application, he observed that all these without a gallant were nothing. Now consider of what has been said, and heaven give you grace to put it in practice.

AMANDA: Alas! Berinthia, did I incline to a gallant (which you know I do not), do you think a man so nice as he could have the least concern for such a plain unpolished thing as I am? It is impossible!

BERINTHIA: Now have you a great mind to put me upon commending you.

AMANDA: Indeed, that was not my design.

BERINTHIA: Nay, if it were, it's all one, for I won't do't; I'll leave that to your looking-glass. But to show you I have some good nature left, I'll commend him, and may be that may do as well.

AMANDA: You have a great mind to persuade me I am in love with him.

BERINTHIA: I have a great mind to persuade you, you don't know what you are in love with.

AMANDA: I am sure I am not in love with him, nor never shall be, so let that pass. But you were saying something you would commend him for.

BERINTHIA: Oh, you'd be glad to hear a good character of him, however.

AMANDA: Psha!

BERINTHIA: Psha!—Well, 'tis a foolish undertaking for women in these kinds of matters to pretend to deceive one another.—Have not I been bred a woman as well as you?

AMANDA: What then?

BERINTHIA: Why, then I understand my trade so well, that whenever I am told of a man I like, I cry, Psha! But that I may spare you the pains of putting me a second time in mind to commend him, I'll proceed, and give you this account of him. That though 'tis possible he may have had women with as good faces as your ladyship's (no discredit to it either), yet you must know your cautious behavior, with that reserve in your humor, has given him his death's wound. He mortally hates a coquette. He says 'tis impossible to love where we cannot esteem; and that no woman can be esteemed by a man who has sense, if she makes herself cheap in the eye of a fool. That pride to a woman is as necessary as humility to a divine; and that far-fetched and dear- bought, is meat for gentlemen as well as for ladies;—in short, that every woman who has beauty may set a price upon herself, and that by under-selling the market, they ruin the trade. This is his doctrine, how do you like it?

AMANDA: So well, that since I never intend to have a gallant for myself, if I were to recommend one to a friend, he should be the man. (*Enter* WORTHY.) Bless me! He's here, pray heaven he did not hear me.

BERINTHIA: If he did, it won't hurt your reputation; your thoughts are as safe in his heart as in your own.

In this scene, Berinthia is selling the idea of Worthy as a lover to Amanda. Because Berinthia and Loveless are highly attracted to one another, it would be very convenient for them both if Amanda's attention was diverted by a romance on the side. It's not a gossip scene, it is not idle at all; both characters are very actively engaged. It seems to me to stem from the difference of experience each has had of the sexual world. It's a teaching scene. Berinthia tells Amanda: this is what men do, and this is how you handle it. So she is really leading the scene.

The difference between teaching and corruption is quite a fine one. Here there is none of the malevolence one might associate with corruption. The scene seems to have a very joyous feeling. Maybe it is a joyously corrupting scene. Certainly this is a play where the wicked are not punished. Vanbrugh celebrates the life that he is describing. He celebrates all forms of sex. It's the vitality of the activity that he loves.

Berinthia sparkles with activity of mind as well. She is that unusual thing in any society where men are the dominant figures, a witty woman. Jokes and epigrams were regarded as the preserve of men. In Restoration comedy, however, we have several instances of women who have triumphed over that, and who have developed wit. They're generally regarded with suspicion by the other women in the play, because they are playing a man's game. They've learned to duel verbally. The sort of expectation that is aroused when a comic walks on stage is aroused when a witty character walks on. There is something twinkling in the air.

The playful undertow of these texts is very evident here. Berinthia starts off with an invented idea which could have come from any modern writer. She says, in effect, "I've had the most terrible time, I've had to sit still and listen to you being praised for two hours." The witty way she puts it is an immediate signal to Amanda that it's fun; that there's going to be some teasing.

Amanda has to contribute to the sparkle of the scene.

It takes two to tango in wit scenes. If Berinthia is leading, Amanda is following. The person who is following in the dance (and it's always like a dance) is not being *dragged* around the room. He or she is following very actively. Listening is active, not passive. It permits the wit; allows it to flourish; gives it its context. It's a more demanding activity on stage than speaking. (Perhaps in life, too.)

Berinthia seems to preach in this scene. She continues with the image of Worthy as a preacher, taking Amanda's beauty as his text, and concluding—as his moral—that without an admirer she might as well be ugly. This image needs to be held up for our inspection. It needs to be clear to Amanda, and it needs to be clear to the audience. Like Edith Evans as Millamant, you have to float these ideas before us; you have to give each phrase its full value. The world of these characters was much slower than ours; they had time to cogitate, and they had every reason to believe that people were interested in what they had to say. Moreover, the feeling of the age, the temper of the times, as it were, was unhurried. Baroque forms are often exuberant, but never at the expense of form and structure—very different from the more headlong feeling of the Elizabethan period, for example, where the sense of discovery, both psychological and intellectual, both internal and external, was paramount. People of the 17th century *knew*—they weren't finding out. Don't rush on to the conclusion derived from the images in the speech; have the courage to build them to their ending. In plays of this period, there is little sense of characters improvising: they seem always to know what it is they want to say, and the end of sentence almost always clinches the argument. The sentence is thus a sort of arc. If the actor has the whole mental superstructure firmly in his or her mind, then the moral of the sermon will be clear *and* we won't have missed any of the elements. It's an elaborate conceit: don't shortchange us of any of the elaborations. The audience won't lose the thread if the actor holds on to it firmly.

Old actors always say: tell the story, tell the story. That doesn't just mean reveal the action. The images are the story too. The actress playing Berinthia has to characterize the comic idea of a lover leaping into the pulpit to preach a sermon on the beauty of the woman he loves; she has to paint it for us. It's almost like being a cartoonist who draws the text for us to enjoy.

Amanda knows it is a rather elegant joke. She is not shocked by it. Society devolved on people studying each other's behavior and appearance. A virtuoso repertoire of compliments and observations is built up. Amanda doesn't disapprove of or despise the game, the eternal round of conquest. She is not some cold Puritan from the country; in fact, she thinks it's all rather fun, from a distance. She just happens not to want to play the game herself. So while Berinthia has the relish of a games player, Amanda has the relish of an observer. She is not pious, she has her own kind of sexiness, even if she's not ready to jump into bed with anyone except her husband. She is rather fascinated by what goes on. I maintain the whole play is about nothing but sex. It's the presiding concern, and everyone is taken by it one way or the other. So while Amanda's responses are ostensibly quite priggish, actually they demonstrate the desire to know more about Worthy. The humor is in the gap between the subtext, which is her curiosity, and what she actually says.

(Incidentally, when Amanda asks how a man so nice as Worthy could possibly fancy anyone as ordinary as she is, it is an example of a word that has changed its meaning. "Nice" in those days meant discriminating; precise. It's up to the modern actor to transmit the earlier meaning by inflection, or a small fastidious gesture.)

An important factor in playing this scene is that there are no men in it. It's interesting in analyzing this scene to consider how women behave when they are alone together, and how they alter when Worthy comes in. I think that prior to Worthy's entrance, we need a sense of the Turkish bath, of *Steaming*. Both of them mentally let their hair down. Thus, Berinthia points out that between women alone, there is no need for these little formal protestations and pretenses. The only reservation of Amanda's that Berinthia bothers to deal with fully is when she says, there's nothing wrong with your face, it's a perfectly good face, but it's your not being a flirt that really attracts Worthy. She pre-empts Amanda's view that this world of courtship is nothing to do with her by pointing out that in a fashionable world there is always a great premium on the person who dares to be different. The outsider can become oddly, erotically powerful. Amanda is the outsider, and is thunderstruck to realize: *Me?*—the object of this famous gallant's desire? She was all right as long as she felt safely outside the game, but now she is distinctly unsettled.

THE REST

One of the delights of Restoration comedy is the plethora of so-called "character" roles they provide. *The Relapse* is particularly rich in them. In fact, there is scarcely a character that cannot shine, however small it may appear to be. Each of the tradesmen who attends on Foppington in his first scene has a color and a flavor with which to make an impression. I was astonished on re-reading the play to find that the role of the Chaplain, Doctor Bull ("Roger," as the nurse calls him) has no more than ten lines. The actor (Derek Smith) who played the part in the Royal Shakespeare Company's production some twenty years ago made an indelible impression. His performance was a comic masterpiece—and not without tragic overtones. These characters often seem grotesque and exaggerated, and often they are—Coupler is a clear instance—but they are exaggerated *in life*, not merely on the stage. It is crucial to find the reality of these people and not attempt a cartoonlike theatrical stylization. Vanbrugh's comedy, and most of that of the

Restoration, was essentially realistic. Not *naturalistic* at all—there was no question whatever but that we are in a theatre, watching a play—but they always refer to a recognizable reality. The audience, as I say, went to the theatre to see themselves and their contemporaries paraded on stage before them. Coupler may be an exaggeration, but I have no doubt that he existed. We all know people who are preposterous, affected, over-the-top. They're playing to the gallery—in life; and when you play a character like that, you should show that that's how they relate to the other characters on stage, showing off to amuse them, but not—NEVER!—showing off over the other characters' heads, playing directly to the audience in the theatre. Often the clue to the basic characteristic is in the name: Hoyden is clearly lacking in sophistication, Sir Tunbelly Clumsey is a big, unwieldy man. But examination of their texts will reveal that Vanbrugh never sells them short. He never makes fools of them. If anything, they're liable to make fools of those who take them for one.

For an architect and a soldier, whose first play this was, Vanbrugh showed astonishing theatrical consideration, allowing every player wonderful details in the writing in order to establish his thought processes. As I have maintained, it is by their thought processes that ye shall know them, and it is the interlocking and interwinding of many original thought processes that makes *The Relapse* so tonic.

CONCLUSION

"We affirm, in the very act of theatre, the way in which words may transform our whole understanding of life."

As our century has wended its disgraceful way, people have been exposed to less and less demanding media. They have become passive, ceasing to listen or to want to listen. There is no doubt that these plays demand an audience that really listens. But the marvelous thing about Restoration comedy is its tonic effect on the audience's collective brain. If the actors connect with the thoughts and make them dance and leap in the air, then the audience's brain starts to work in the same way.

It's not just a question of being funny. The job of the actors is not to *make* the audience laugh, but to *let* the audience laugh; not to be witty ourselves, but to make the audience witty. If you're around witty people for long enough, your wits start to sharpen. If in the theatre the actors are offering live, vital wit, then the audience will become infected with it too, and a real interplay starts that can make the theatre the most exhilarating place to be in the world.

These plays don't require extra jollification or other kinds of so-called help. I believe modern audiences have been dulled by the sort of director's theatre that offers a lot of music, tremendous amounts of movement and activity, elaborate sets and costumes. All this can be delightful and valuable, but unless at the center of it are actors through whom the vital current of the author's wit is passing, the watcher will be passive, overwhelmed by a tidal wave of stimulation. We actors must work with total clarity to give back to mere words their true potency. The theatre is really the last bastion of the spoken word. Like the monks in Ireland who—during the Dark Ages—kept learning alive, actors can preserve the miracle of language. Every time an actor makes you hear a word and understand it as if for the first time, the miracle has happened again. No other medium cares so much about language.

In the theatre we can never stop asking what words mean, how they are being used, what they tell us about the characters and their times. We affirm, in the very act of theatre, the way in which words may transform our whole understanding of life. In performing these plays with full belief in their unvarnished vitality, therefore, we are celebrating aspects of the human condition that are in danger of being lost in the modern world. That is the theatre's business: the giving and restoring of life. And these plays contain—if we will only trust them— as abundant and brilliant life as any written.

BIOGRAPHICAL NOTE ON THE AUTHOR

Simon Callow studied at the Queen's University of Belfast and trained as an actor at the Drama Centre of London. He has played on stage in the London fringe, the National Theatre and the West End in many productions including *Kiss of the Spider Woman*, *Amadeus*, *Galileo*, *As You Like It*, *The Beastly Beatitudes of Balthasar B*, *Total Eclipse*, the two-part *Faust* playing the title role, and *The Relapse* as Lord Foppington; in films including *Amadeus*, *A Room With a View*, *Maurice*, and *Manifesto*, *Mr and Mrs Bridge* and *Postcards from the Edge*; and in television playing Mr Micawber in *David Copperfield*, Raimondi in *Cariani and the Courtesans*, Quass in *Simon Gray's Old Flames*, and the title part in his own comedy series, *Chance in a Million*.

As director, his productions include *Cosi fan Tutte*, *Die Fledermaus*, *Jacques and His Master* (which he also translated from the work by Milan Kundera), the original production, both for London and Broadway, of Willy Russell's *Shirley Valentine*, *The Infernal Machine* with Maggie Smith, and *Single Spies* by Alan Bennett for the National Theatre. He directed the film of *The Ballad of the Sad Cafe* with Vanessa Redgrave and Rod Steiger. Callow, fluent in French, has translated several plays for production, and is author of *Being an Actor*, *Charles Laughton: a Difficult Actor*, and *Shooting the Actor*, the journal of his experience acting in Dusan Makavejev's film *Manifesto*.

SOLILOQUY!
The Shakespeare Monologues
Edited by Michael Earley and Philippa Keil

At last, over 175 of Shakespeare's finest and most performable monologues taken from all 37 plays are here in two easy-to-use volumes (MEN and WOMEN). Selections travel the entire spectrum of the great dramatist's vision, from comedies and romances to tragedies, pathos and histories.

"SOLILOQUY is an excellent and comprehensive collection of Shakespeare's speeches. Not only are the monologues wide-ranging and varied, but they are superbly annotated. Each volume is prefaced by an informative and reassuring introduction, which explains the signals and signposts by which Shakespeare helps the actor on his journey through the text. It includes a very good explanation of blank verse, with excellent examples of irregularities which are specifically related to character and acting intentions. These two books are a must for any actor in search of a 'classical' audition piece."

ELIZABETH SMITH
Head of Voice & Speech
The Juilliard School

paper • MEN: ISBN 0-936839-78-3 • WOMEN: ISBN 0-936839-79-1

SHAKESCENES
SHAKESPEARE FOR TWO
Edited with an Introduction
by John Russell Brown

Shakespeare's plays are not the preserve of "Shakespearean Actors" who specialize in a remote species of dramatic life. John Russell Brown offers guidance for those who have little or no experience with the formidable Bard in both the Introduction and Advice to Actors, and in the notes to each of the thirty-five scenes.

The scenes are presented in newly-edited texts, with notes which clarify meanings, topical references, puns, ambiguities, etc. Each scene has been chosen for its independent life requiring only the simplest of stage properties and the barest of spaces. A brief description of characters and situation prefaces each scene, and is followed by a commentary which discusses its major acting challenges and opportunities.

Shakescenes are for small classes and large workshops, and for individual study whenever two actors have the opportunity to work together.

From the Introduction:

"Of course, a way of speaking a character's lines meaningfully and clearly must be found, but that alone will not bring any play to life. Shakespeare did not write for talking heads ... Actors need to be acutely present all the time; ... they are like boxers in a ring, who dare not lose concentration or the ability to perform at full power for fear of losing consciousness altogether."

paper • ISBN: 1-55783-049-5

ON SINGING ONSTAGE
New, Completely Revised Edition
by David Craig

"David Craig knows more about singing in the musical theatre than anyone in this country — which probably means in the world. Time and time again his advice and training have resulted in actors moving from non-musical theatre into musicals with ease and expertise. Short of taking his classes, this book is a must."

HAROLD PRINCE

In the New and Revised *On Singing Onstage* David Craig presents the same technique he has given to America's leading actors, actresses and dancers over the past thirty years. By listing the do's and don'ts of all aspects of singing onstage, you will be brought closer to the discovery of your own personal "style." That achievement plus information on how to get the most mileage out of an audition (what to sing and how to choose it) makes this book an indispensably practical self-teaching tool.

For anyone who has to (or wants to) sing anywhere, from amateur productions to the Broadway stage, *On Singing Onstage* is an essential guide for making the most of your talent.

AMONG DAVID CRAIG'S STUDENTS:

Carol Burnett, Cyd Charisse, James Coco, Sally Field, Lee Grant, Valerie Harper, Barbara Harris, Rock Hudson, Sally Kellerman, Jack Klugman, Cloris Leachman, Roddy McDowell, Marsha Mason, Anthony Perkins, Lee Remick, Eva Marie Saint, Marlo Thomas, Cicely Tyson, Nancy Walker . . . and many more.

paper • ISBN: 1-55783-043-6

❤APPLAUSE❤

THE STANISLAVSKY TECHNIQUE: RUSSIA
A Workbook for Actors
by Mel Gordon

"Without exaggeration, the Stanislavsky system has needed Mel Gordon's book for over fifty years . . . the most original and useful research by an American on our theatre's richest artistic heritage."

ROBERT ELLERMAN
Performink

Stop reading about Stanislavsky and wondering what it's all supposed to mean. Meet the master and his disciples as they evolve new techniques and exercises in a workshop atmosphere during a quarter of a century.

This volume covers:

THE STANISLAVSKY SYSTEM
First Studio Exercises 1912-1916

VAKHTANGOV AS REBEL AND THEORETICIAN
Exercises 1919-1921

MICHAEL CHEKHOV
Exercises 1919-1952

STANISLAVSKY'S FOURTH PERIOD
Theory of Physical Actions: 1934-1938

paper • ISBN: 0-936839-08-2

LIFE IS A DREAM
AND OTHER SPANISH CLASSICS
Edited by Eric Bentley
Translated by Roy Campbell

"The name of Eric Bentley is enough to guarantee the significance of any book of or about drama."

—Robert Penn Warren

LIFE IS A DREAM
by Calderon de la Barca

FUENTE OVEJUNA
by Lope de Vega

THE TRICKSTER OF SEVILLE
by Tirso de Molina

THE SIEGE OF NUMANTIA
by Miguel de Cervantes

paper • ISBN: 1-55783-006-1   cloth • ISBN: 1-55783-005-3

THE MISANTHROPE
AND OTHER FRENCH CLASSICS
Edited by Eric Bentley

"I would recommend Eric Bentley's collection to all who really care for theatre."

—Harold Clurman

THE MISANTHROPE
by Molière
English version by Richard Wilbur

PHAEDRA
by Racine
English version by Robert Lowell

THE CID
by Corneille
English version by James Schevill

FIGARO'S MARRIAGE
by Beaumarchais
English version by Jacques Barzun

paper • ISBN: 0-936839-19-8

THE MISER
and
GEORGE DANDIN
by Molière
Translated by Albert Bermel

Harpagon, the most desperate, scheming miser in literature, starves his servants, declines to pay them, cheats his own children if he can save (or make) a few coins, and when his hoard of gold disappears, insanely accuses himself of being the thief.

Dandin, in this rousing classic, not previously available in English for sixty years, is a man in a plight that everybody but him will find entertaining.

paper • ISBN: 0-936839-75-9

SCAPIN
and
DON JUAN
by Molière
Translated by Albert Bermel

In one of Molière's most popular plays, Scapin, that monarch of con men, puts his endless store of ingenuity to work, getting two lovesick young men married to the girls they pine for and, along the way, taking revenge on their grasping old fathers.

Closed down after its first, highly successful run because of opposition from powerful enemies of the playwright, *Don Juan* was performed in a bowdlerized version for almost two hundred years, until actors, directors and critics restored the original text, recognizing it as the most ambitious and mightiest of Molière's prose plays

paper • ISBN: 0-936839-80-5

APPLAUSE

IN SEARCH
OF THEATER

by
Eric Bentley

First published in 1953, *In Search of Theater* is wide-ly regarded as the standard portrait of the Euro-pean and American theater in the turbulent and seminal years following World War II. The book's influence contributed substantially to the rising reputations of such artists as Bertolt Brecht, Charles Champlin and Martha Graham.

"The most erudite and intelligent living writing on the theatre." —**Ronald Bryden**
THE NEW STATESMAN

"Certainly America's foremost theatre critic . . ."
—**Irving Wardle**
THE TIMES

paper • ISBN: 1-55783-111-4

RECYCLING SHAKESPEARE
by Charles Marowitz

Marowitz' irreverent approach to the bard is destined to outrage Shakespearean scholars across the globe. Marowitz rejects the notion that a "classic" is a sacrosanct entity fixed in time and bounded by its text. A living classic, according to Marowitz, should provoke lively response—even indignation!

In the same way that Shakespeare himself continued to meditate and transform his own ideas and the shape they took, Marowitz gives us license to continue that meditation in productions extrapolated from Shakespeare's work. Shakespeare becomes the greatest of all catalysts who stimulates a constant reformulation of the fundamental questions of philosophy, history and meaning.

Marowitz introduces us to Shakespeare as an active contemporary collaborator who strives with us to yield a vibrant contemporary theatre. To the author, Shakespeare is like a prism in which "I discern innumerable reflections of myself and my society, and like a prism, it refracts many pinpoints of color—rather than transmitting one unbroken light."

Charles Marowitz, a close collaborator with Peter Brook at the Royal Shakespeare Company, was for over a decade the artistic director of London's Open Space Theatre.

paper • ISBN: 1-55783-094-0   cloth • ISBN: 1-55783-093-2

APPLAUSE

STANISLAVSKI REVEALED
by Sonia Moore

Other than Stanislavski's own published work, the most widely read interpretation of his techniques remains Sonia Moore's pioneering study, *The Stanislavski System*. Sonia Moore is on the frontier again now as she reveals the subtle tissue of ideas behind what Stanislavski regarded as his "major breakthrough," the Method of Physical Actions. Moore has devoted the last decade in her world-famous studio to an investigation of Stanislavski's final technique. The result is the first detailed discussion of Moore's own theory of psychophysical unity which she has based on her intensive practical meditation on Stanislavski's consummate conclusions about acting.

Demolishing the popular notion that his methods depend on private—self-centered—expression, Moore now reveals Stanislavski as the advocate of deliberate, controlled, conscious technique—internal and external at the same time—a technique that makes tremendous demands on actors but that rewards them with the priceless gift of creative life.

Stanislavski Revealed is a completely revised and updated re-assessment of Moore's classic book *Training an Actor*. In addition to detailed descriptions of the exercises she employs in her studio, she now extends Stanislavski's insights to enable playwrights and directors to benefit from his technique.

paper • ISBN: 1-55783-103-3

ONE-ACT COMEDIES OF MOLIÈRE

Translated by Albert Bermel

- *THE JEALOUS HUSBAND* -
- *THE FLYING DOCTOR* -
- *TWO PRECIOUS MAIDENS RIDICULED* -
- *THE IMAGINARY CUCKOLD* -
- *THE REHEARSAL AT VERSAILLES* -
- *THE FORCED MARRIAGE* -
- *THE SEDUCTIVE MISTRESS* -

These are the best of Molière's masterful one-acts, blending broad farce and pointed wit to express his never-ending delight in human foibles.

But Molière is more than just the "master of the laugh," as Albert Bermel writes in the introduction. For behind the comic words and gestures of these matchless rogues, tightfisted masters, possessive lovers and elegant ladies lurk fears and insecurities and their consequences. In Molière, yes, in truth, there are many kinds of laughter.

"Bermel's Molière translations are, with those of Richard Wilbur, by far the most amusing we have." —Eric Bentley

paper • ISBN: 1-55783-109-2

THE LIFE OF THE DRAMA
by Eric Bentley

" ... Eric Bentley's radical new look at the grammar of theatre ... is a work of exceptional virtue, and readers who find more in it to disagree with than I do will still, I think, want to call it central, indispensable. ... The book justifies its title by being precisely about the ways in which life manifests itself in the theatre. ... If you see any crucial interest in such topics as the death of Cordelia, Godot's non-arrival ... this is a book to be read and read again." —**Frank Kermode**
THE NEW YORK REVIEW OF BOOKS

"*The Life of the Drama* ... is a remarkable exploration of the roots and bases of dramatic art, the most far-reaching and revelatory we have had."
—**Richard Gilman**
BOOK WEEK

"*The Life of the Drama* is Eric Bentley's magnum opus or to put it more modestly his best book. I might call it an esthetic of the drama, but this again sounds ponderous; the book is eminently lucid and often helpfully epigrammatic. Everyone genuinely interested in the theatre should read it. It is full of remarkable insights into many of the most important plays ever written."
—**Harold Clurman**

paper • ISBN: 1-55783-110-6

MICHAEL CHEKHOV:
On Theater and the Art of Acting
by Michael Chekhov
Edited & with a 48-page Course Guide by Mala Powers

For the first time in over 30 years, Michael Chekhov—acting guru to Marilyn Monroe, Anthony Quinn, Gregory Peck and dozens of other major theater and film stars—is taking on new students! Join the legendary teacher/director, heralded as Russia's greatest actor, for a six-hour master class on the fundamentals of the Chekhov technique:

- The Art of Characterization
- Short Cuts to Role Preparation
- How to Awaken Artistic Feelings and Emotions
- Avoiding Monotony in Performance
- Overcoming Inhibitions and Building Self-Confidence
- Psycho-physical Exercises
- Development of the Ensemble Spirit

"Michael Chekhov remains the most inspiring director-teacher I have ever worked with." —Anthony Quinn

paper • ISBN: 1-55783-117-3

DIRECTING THE ACTION
by Charles Marowitz

Every actor and director who enters the orbit of this major work will find himself challenged to a deeper understanding of his art and propelled into further realms of exploration. Marowitz meditates on all the sacred precepts of theater practice including auditions, casting, design, rehearsal, actor psychology, dramaturgy and the text.

Directing the Action yields a revised liturgy for all those who would celebrate a theatrical passion on today's stage. But in order to be a disciple in this order, the theater artist must be poised toward piety and heresy at once. Not since Peter Brook's *The Empty Space* has a major director of such international stature confronted the ancient dilemmas of the stage with such a determined sense of opportunity and discovery.

"An enerbizing, uplifting work ... reading Marowitz on theater is like reading heroic fiction in an age without heroes."
—LOS ANGELES WEEKLY

"A cogent and incisive collection of ideas, well formulated and clearly set forth; an important contribution on directing in a postmodern theater." —CHOICE

"Consistently thought-provoking ... Sure to be controversial."
—LIBRARY JOURNAL

paper • ISBN: 1-55783-072-X

From the APPLAUSE

60-minute videocassettes based o

ACTING IN OPERA
Jonathan Miller

"Through the climactic scene of *La Traviata*, the good doctor clowned, interpreted, gestured and flung his eminently quotable metaphors at us and a performance began miraculously to take shape. The problem for singers is that opera is difficult enough as music, let alone as stagecraft. ... Miller cajoled, joked, visibly eased tensions between contending forces, provided props, explained nuances. The dying, he memorably told the cast, spend all their time consoling the living. And by the end, drama had emerged from opera. Magic, underpinned by a great deal of hard work."

—THE LISTENER

ISBN 1-55783-036-3

ACTING IN
SHAKESPEAREAN COMEDY
Janet Suzman

"Suzman is a major classical actress ... she is also a born teacher ... Beneath her flame-colored hair, Suzman burned, and her students duly caught fire ... she persistently came out with striking, stimulating remarks [with] workshop snippets of *Much Ado*, *As you Like It*, and *Twelfth Night*."

—**Benedict Nightingale**
LONDON TIMES

ISBN 1-55783-115-7

VIDEO LIBRARY
he BBC Acting Master Class Series

ACTING IN TRAGEDY
Brian Cox

"Tragedy. A rollicking good time he has with it too—menacing whispers, daggers and blood obviously have their funny side, at least with his fascinated young audience."

—DAILY MAIL

"Full of common sense ... In the end, it is we actors who are on the spot ... Scenes that start rehearsal as straighforward Shakespeare babble assume dramatic shape ..."

—THE TIMES (London)

ISBN 1-55783-114-9

ACTING IN HIGH COMEDY
Maria Aitken

"A lively session on high comedy, with examples from Coawrd, Wilde, Sheridan and Congreve ... [revealing] the spark that tramsforms a routine reading into a vibrant one in a scene from *Private Lives* which by the time Aitken has finished with it has attained something close to brilliance."

—THE TIMES (London)

ISBN 1-55783-116-5

THE MICHAEL CAINE VIDEO

60-minute VHS Videocassette
Based on the BBC Acting Master Class Series

ACTING IN FILM
by MICHAEL CAINE

"Remarkable material ... A grand entertainment, with more drama than most movies ..."

—Gene Siskel
SISKEL & EBERT

"I'm not going to look at a movie the same way again. ... It will probably change the way you look at whatever movie you rented ..."

—Roger Ebert
SISKEL & EBERT

"A delightful account by the actor of what life and death on a move set, in terms of career, are like ... Fresh, funny and informative ..."

—Bruce Eder
THE VILLAGE VOICE

"An indispensable tape ... This is for anybody who cares about movies."

—Michael Medved
SNEAK PREVIEWS GOES VIDEO

ISBN: 1-55783-034-7

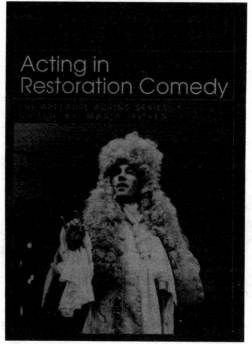